First Steps in
SAP® Predictive
Analytics

Anurag Barua

Thank you for purchasing this book from Espresso Tutorials!

Like a cup of espresso coffee, Espresso Tutorials SAP books are concise and effective. We know that your time is valuable and we deliver information in a succinct and straightforward manner. It only takes our readers a short amount of time to consume SAP concepts. Our books are well recognized in the industry for leveraging tutorial-style instruction and videos to show you step by step how to successfully work with SAP.

Check out our YouTube channel to watch our videos at *https://www.youtube.com/user/EspressoTutorials*.

If you are interested in SAP Finance and Controlling, join us at http://www.fico-forum.com/forum2/ to get your SAP questions answered and contribute to discussions.

Related titles from Espresso Tutorials:

► Wolfgang Niefert: Business Intelligence with SAP® BI Edge
  http://4040.espresso-tutorials.com

► Kermit Bravo & Scott Cairncross: SAP® Enterprise Performance Management (EPM) Add-In
  http://5042.espresso-tutorials.com

► Gerardo di Giuseppe: First Steps in SAP® Business Warehouse (BW)
  http://5088.espresso-tutorials.com

► Jörg Böke: SAP® BI Analysis Office – a Practical Guide
  http://5096.espresso-tutorials.com

► Rob Frye, Joe Darlak, Dr. Bjarne Berg: The SAP® BW to HANA Migration Handbook
  http://5109.espresso-tutorials.com

► Christian Savelli: SAP® BW on SAP HANA
  http://5128.espresso-tutorials.com

► Deepa Rawat: Practical Guide to Advanced DSOs in SAP®
  http://5213.espresso-tutorials.com

► Frank Riesner, Klaus-Peter Sauer: SAP® BW/4HANA and BW on HANA
  http://5215.espresso-tutorials.com

Anurag Barua
First Steps in SAP® Predictive Analytics

ISBN: 978-3-96012-846-5

Editor: Lisa Jackson

Cover Design: Philip Esch

Cover Photo: © istockphoto.com | RichVintage # 864707740

Interior Design: Johann-Christian Hanke

Feedback
We greatly appreciate any feedback you may have concerning this book. Please send your feedback via email to: *info@espresso-tutorials.com*.

Table of Contents

Foreword		**7**
1	**Analytics: The journey so far**	**11**
	1.1 Analytics: An overview and timeline	12
	1.2 The best years lie ahead	17
2	**SAP PA: High-level overview**	**19**
	2.1 Introduction to SAP PA	20
	2.2 History and evolution of SAP PA	21
	2.3 SAP PA architecture and technical components	23
	2.4 SAP PA with SAP HANA	24
	2.5 SAP PA in SAP's BI roadmap	27
	2.6 Installation	29
3	**Core components and units**	**35**
	3.1 Data manager	35
	3.2 Performing an event log aggregation	38
	3.3 Performing a text analysis	43
	3.4 Automated analytics	49
	3.5 Expert analytics	81
	3.6 Toolkit	109
4	**Predictive analytics: Use cases**	**123**
	4.1 Use case: Sales/pipeline forecasting	125
5	**Conclusion**	**161**
6	**References**	**163**
	6.1 Websites	163
	6.2 YouTube videos	165

A   The Author   **170**

B   Index   **171**

C   Disclaimer   **173**

Foreword

Ever since Adam and Eve took a bite of the forbidden apple, human beings have been endowed with the ability to look back, analyze their actions, and be introspective. But for most of the first two millennia, the ability to look forward to make meaningful and realistic projections (if not predictions) about the future was limited. Limited in the context of data. Since the first half of the 20th century, computing was in an inchoate state, processing of data to do historical analysis itself was limited both in volume and speed. The second half of the 20th century saw an explosion in technical innovation, on both the hardware and software fronts, thus making historical analysis commonplace and providing the connected masses with ever-cheaper and faster ways to utilize the data universe to make meaningful and realistic projections.

Let's ponder on how certain mundane activities that are built on analytics have evolved over time. The first one that comes to mind is weather prediction. A few decades ago, predicting the weather was limited to a generalized summary replete with clichés like "alternating periods of sunshine and rain", "cooler in the evening", etc., and limited to a day or two. The ability to predict severe weather patterns, such as hurricanes, with a reasonable degree of accuracy was also limited. Thanks to predictive analytics (and of course all the technological innovations that have enabled it), you can now get weather predictions for at least a week or two that are mostly accurate and frequent (hourly). Predictive analytics vis-à-vis weather is so intertwined with our daily lives that we pause to notice it only when a snowstorm dumps fewer inches of snow than predicted or a hurricane veers slightly off course. But thanks to the power of predictive analytics, most of the world is better equipped to handle the fury of Mother Nature in a way it simply wasn't able to even a couple of decades ago. In the U.S., by accurately predicting the path of hurricanes, predictive analytics has saved countless lives by providing early warnings and allowing those in the paths of such hurricanes the timely ability to take remedial action, including evacuation in the worst case.

Another excellent use case of predictive analytics is customer segmentation and analysis. In this era of globalization, competition to not only retain your customer base but also expand it has become a mission statement. The intensity of this competition is directly proportional to uniqueness of the product. If you sell airplanes, you are in a small group of competitors and customer churn is probably not very realistic. However, if you sell a commodity product like toothpaste, where margins are low and competition is intense, predictive analytics can be used to understand the various categories your customers can be grouped in, and help you analyze and plan where you should go for your next set of customers. How is that possible? When you observe some common characteristics (such as demographics, economics, etc.) that bind buyers to your brand of toothpaste, you can plan on targeting groups exhibiting the same characteristics in different geographies. Or if the toothpaste maker is interested in launching a new type of toothpaste, predictive analytics comes in equally handy in determining where it would be most effective to launch a new product.

Another popular area for predictive analytics is supply chain – planning, forecasting, and execution. The ultra-connected nature of our global economy coupled with the outsourcing of manufacturing to low-cost countries has created incredible complexities in a multinational's supply chain. Small glitches can cause major disruptions and once that happens, the ripple effects compound quickly. However, by using data science and predictive analytics, you can do some fairly accurate forecasting of demand to help you maintain adequate inventory levels, among other things. This can lead to speedy fulfilment of customer demand and higher customer satisfaction.

Another very common use case for predictive analytics in the supply chain is in predictive maintenance. A traditional view of maintenance is the preventative maintenance of machinery, i.e. some part of your machinery breaks and you maintain or fix it. But what if the parts are not readily available? You can end up with longer downtime, which could be detrimental to production and have a direct impact on your bottom line, not to mention lower customer satisfaction. Using predictive analytics, the Internet of Things (IoT), and data science, you can quickly pivot from preventative to predictive maintenance. Sensors embedded in these machines collect data on all key performance indicators (KPIs) in real time to keep track of how well every part is working and how soon each is about to fail. This serves as an early warning so the parts can be procured in a proactive manner. This can ultimately lead to increased customer satisfaction by enabling production schedules to be met and order fulfilment to be done in a timely manner.

I can keep going on and on about how predictive analytics is being utilized in commonplace and exotic ways, but you get the point. Predictive analytics is ubiquitous and technological innovations and improvements are continuously making it more and more mainstream.

So back to my opening statement on Adam, Eve, and the forbidden apple. What would they do today? They would step into the Garden of Eden well-armed with analytics on which tree to approach (and not necessarily the Tree of Life) for maximizing knowledge and which fruit to take a bite of.

The purpose of this book is to introduce you to SAP Predictive Analytics, primarily from the perspective of the regular business user and secondarily from that of the analyst and/or data scientist. As a regular/casual business user, you are likely to come across terminology that might be somewhat alien. I would encourage you to give it your full attention because such terminology and sophisticated technology (primarily in the form of data mining algorithms) forms the foundation of predictive analytics. If you are a data scientist or an analyst, some of the terms and concepts are likely to sound familiar—I hope it will inform and reinforce what you already know.

Happy reading!

We have added a few icons to highlight important information. These include:

Tips

Tips highlight information that provides more details about the subject being described and/or additional background information.

Attention

Attention notices highlight information that you should be aware of when you go through the examples in this book on your own.

Finally, a note concerning the copyright: all screenshots printed in this book are the copyright of SAP SE. All rights are reserved by SAP SE. Copyright pertains to all SAP images in this publication. For the sake of simplicity, we do not mention this specifically underneath every screenshot.

1 Analytics: The journey so far

What is predictive analytics? To answer that question we need to step back in time to understand the evolution of analytics. The first generation of computing was all about using computers for automating operational tasks. What is meant by operational? Basically, entering data through terminals, running the data through computer programs and algorithms (or crunching), and completing a task faster than a whole lot of human beings could do either individually or as a group. So, for example, if a booking agent wanted to book a ticket for an airline passenger, the agent would enter all the search criteria through a computer terminal, then the elephant-sized mainframe computer would run a bunch of programs and let the agent know what was available. Once the agent found the right match, they would carry out the transaction and purchase the ticket for the passenger by interacting with the computer through the terminal and then print the ticket on a printer.

With the increasing processing power of computers, along with their ability to store increasing amounts of data (not necessarily in lockstep), there was an exponential rise in their usage for advanced computing, such as in research and development (think of agencies like the Defense Advanced Research Projects Agency (DARPA) where the concept of the Internet was first conceived—or CERN, where the innovation of email was first conceived), aerospace, automobiles, etc. The era of the supercomputer enabled these giants to use computers for highly sophisticated operational tasks such as controlling all the dynamics of airplanes, rockets, etc. Even so, all of this was still very operational. You would feed the computer data and get the results simply based on the data you provided. There was no need or possibility of utilizing historical data or any past information. It was all about the present or the near-present. And indeed, that is what operational processing is all about. However, even as all these advances were going on, there was another movement that was gaining momentum— using computers for analytical processing. And contrary to conventional wisdom, analytical processing did not begin with the personal computer (PC) era and certainly not with the smart phone era. What we understand by *analytics* has been in existence for over 70 years.

1.1 Analytics: An overview and timeline

Before I proceed, let me define what analytics or analytical computing is all about. Analytical computing (as opposed to operational computing), in its simplest rendition, is about using large volumes of data (generally historical in nature—anywhere from a year or more old) to detect trends, patterns, or anomalies and make better decisions. Analytics is at the heart of what used to be called a decision support system (DSS)—a term that is teetering on the brink of obsolescence today due to the ubiquity of analytics.

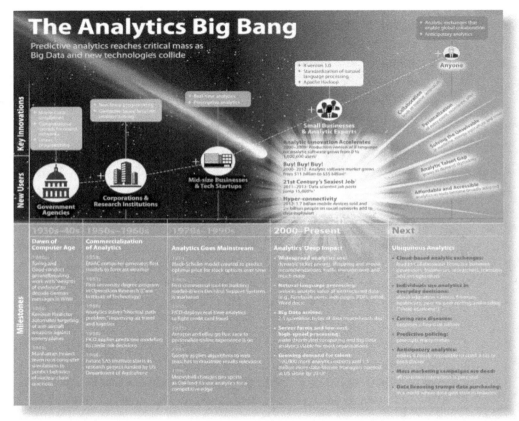

Figure 1.1: Analytics timeline (Source: https://www.fico.com/en/latest-thinking/infographic/the-analytics-big-bang)

1.1.1 The early years

The infographic shown in Figure 1.1 gives a good sense of how analytics has evolved over the past seven to eight decades. And it explodes the myth that analytics is a recent innovation. Probably the first documented foray into analytics was in 1944 with the Manhattan Project. The team ran computer simulations to predict the behavior of nuclear reactions. Needless to say, it was rare in those days to use computers for analytics primarily because computers and computing technology was in an embryonic state and was still in the realm of science fiction. The fifties and the sixties benefitted tremendously from advances made in computer science (in both hardware and software areas) and the ENIAC (the most powerful computer in its day) was able to carry out simulations of weather models and make weather predictions. It was also in the sixties that sophisticated software algorithms were able to generate the answer to the shortest path between any two points, thereby leading to optimization of logistics and air travel. However, the technology revolution hadn't yet taken off. Computers were still defined by their size—the bigger, the better—and due to their prohibitive cost it was only the biggest of companies and research organizations (that had generous funding from their primary benefactors, generally the government) that seemed to have a stranglehold on these amazing machines.

1.1.2 The preteens

The computing revolution truly took off in the seventies as Moore's Law manifested itself not only in the inverse relationship between processing speed and size of the processor, but also in the rapidly plummeting cost of computers. A slew of computing technologies went mainstream, including personal computing that ensured that the digital divide between the haves and have-nots would rapidly shrink, if not vanish. It also ensured a steady transition in big corporations from mainframes to personal computing that rapidly expanded overall computing capabilities of an organization. Midsize and small companies that were excluded from the computing race could now afford to buy computers. And three companies that did not even exist in the sixties came to establish themselves as forces to be reckoned with: Microsoft, SAP, and Oracle. However, none of these had much of a role to play in the analytics realm in their early days. Microsoft was trying to corner the market for operating systems and office computing, SAP had just virtually started a new category (enterprise resource planning, or ERP), and Oracle had databases and database management in its sights.

Advances in analytics were not very widespread during the seventies and eighties (barring some research-oriented heavy-duty analytics), the value of a DSS and the role that analytical computing played in a DSS were established. The challenge was that the demand for analytics was neither particularly dominant nor were companies willing to sacrifice their operational needs for the still somewhat vague notion of analytics.

1.1.3   The teens and early adulthood

As we entered the nineties, devices got smaller, faster, smarter, and cheaper. The rapid availability of the Internet during this decade virtually guaranteed that computing and connectivity had almost become synonymous. Organizations and people had access to all kinds of data. The data being generated was growing at a colossal rate, which made organizations and people more knowledgeable since all this data could be crunched or mined to make them smarter. Enter analytics...During the nineties, upstarts such as Amazon, eBay, and Google (to a limited extent) started using analytics to get a better understanding of people's buying habits to tailor their offerings appropriately and to also use the collected data to make predictions of what consumers might be interested in buying in the future.

Meanwhile, SAP, Oracle, and Microsoft had become behemoths in their respective areas. While SAP strode the world of ERP as a colossus, Oracle became the undisputed master of relational databases, and Microsoft had captured not only the operating system market with Windows but also the business applications market with its Microsoft Office suite. IBM was still one of the original giants and it was doing a slew of things in both hardware and software. It's important to note that none of these giants were taking a serious look at data warehousing, business intelligence, or analytics. At best, they were casually flirting with the idea of analytics. But some visionary companies that did not have to deal with any of the commercial and legacy-imposed burdens had started making strong forays into the world of analytics like SAS, Microstrategy, Tableau, BusinessObjects, etc. Their quickly expanding bases established that the analytics market was on the cusp of a boom.

1.1.4 Coming of age

As we entered the new millennium, the entire IT industry was on a tear and things were changing at a dizzying speed. Consider all the *disruptive innovations* of the first few years of the new millennium:

▶ **Connectivity to the Internet** had become commonplace in the developed world with the developing nations taking big strides. The era of the dial-up (and thus slow downloads and long waits) was practically over and connectivity was accelerating rapidly. Advances in networking technology, epitomized by broadband cable and Wi-Fi, made it easier for large volumes of data to be streamed in real time with rapidly decreasing incidences of buffering.

▶ The **PC revolution** had yielded to the laptop era, which itself was in danger of losing its preeminent position to smart devices like smart phones and tablets. The rapid advance in mobility has had tremendous implications—it has spawned the 'app' economy, geographical barriers have generally crumbled, and data about conceivably anything you care to know about is a tap or finger-swipe away.

▶ The venerable **Moore's Law** was still proving itself true and computing and storage prices were dropping even faster. In the realm of storage, innovations such as in-memory computing and advanced compression algorithms combined to make it easier to store massive volumes of data.

▶ **Grid computing** (initially championed by IBM) and cloud computing (with Amazon taking the lead) was widely being embraced by a variety of enterprises. This trend ensured that availability to world-class computing capabilities on demand was just a credit card swipe away.

▶ Although the late nineties saw a spike in **collaboration and social networking** in the form of chat rooms, the lack of bandwidth and limited coverage of the Internet kept this industry shackled. With the rapid rise of connectivity both in terms of speed and coverage, collaboration and social networking started growing exponentially. The initial years of the new millennium saw the emergence of upstarts like MySpace (now defunct), LinkedIn, and some less heralded ones like Second Life and Del.icio.us. Then came Facebook and Twitter, names that are now practically synonymous with social media. Then came Spotify, Instagram, Snapchat, and

Whatsapp. These are some of the more well-known names. There are many other large non-U.S.-based social media apps such as (now acquired) Orkut, WeChat, and Sina Weibo. Suffice it to say that if you are connected to the Internet in some shape or form, you are a social networker.

▶ The **global economy** had integrated to such an extent that technology made all physical boundaries meaningless, global supply chains had become the norm, and competition was so intense that you had to react almost instantaneously to a certain situation (planned or unplanned) to sustain your competitive edge. While transaction processing applications were still necessary, it was no longer sufficient for companies to do data analysis with such applications.

What exactly is the key message that emerges from the convergence of these trends?

1. We are inundated by data coming at us in all directions in all shapes and forms. It is only likely to get even more relentless. Today's Big Data could seem puny in comparison to the growth in volume, velocity, and variety a few months from now.

2. The expectation that we (whether as individuals or enterprises) should be able to make sense of this data in real time has almost become a right. With the ever-increasing access to cheap, but extremely powerful computing resources, software applications need to seamlessly incorporate analytics capabilities into their offerings.

3. Although historical or prescriptive analysis is important insofar as it helps explain what went right or wrong, it is equally (if not more) important to make reasonable projections (if not predictions) for the future (predictive analytics).

4. Data analytics cannot just be the prerogative of data scientists. The fruits of data analytics need to be enjoyed by everyone in the enterprise from entry through executive levels regardless of technical expertise. Data analytics needs to be a commodity that is made available to consumers (and maybe with some effort from the data scientists) on demand.

1.2   The best years lie ahead

It is no cliché to say that the future is data science and analytics. Edwards Deming had once famously said, "In God we trust, all others bring data." I would extend that to suggest that even God possibly trusts data. The power that any person or entity wields in this world has a clear co-relation to how they analyze the vast volumes of relevant data at their disposal. With some nascent technologies establishing themselves strongly, such as artificial intelligence, machine learning, data mining, natural language processing, and Big Data, we will be witnessing an explosive growth in this field. The use cases for analytics will straddle the gamut from trivial (such as what brand of napkins would be the best choice for a family of four) to critical (such as KPIs of a driverless car), and everything in between. As analytics becomes a commodity, it is not inconceivable that it will be treated like a utility (such as electricity) and will become an inseparable part of our lives. It will become an empowering and uplifting force that will, in time, make our world a smarter place to live.

2 SAP PA: High-level overview

Now that you have an understanding and appreciation for the importance of predictive analytics, let's explore SAP Predictive Analytics
(SAP PA). It is SAP's premier application for providing you (regardless
of whether you are a regular user or a data scientist) with the ability to
make projections about future events based on its ability to mine data
sets to unearth trends, patterns, and relationships. SAP PA is an advanced business intelligence (BI) tool that helps you combine the past
(hindsight) with the current (insight) to gain knowledge/information
(foresight) so that you can make smarter business decisions. Such
smarter business decisions include staying ahead of your competition, reducing costs by eliminating waste, gaining efficiencies by fine-
tuning operations, and making investments in the right areas. SAP PA
enables easy analytics by incorporating advanced visualization capabilities.

SAP PA is a natural outgrowth to conventional (prescriptive) analytics
which tends to heavily focus on history. I have worked with many SAP
customers who are either dipping their toes into SAP PA after having established a conventional BI/analytics framework that provides them with
a dependable window into the past, or are thinking ahead and wanting to
leverage the tremendous value hidden in their data to be smarter about
the future. I tend to use this simple analogy: when you invest into your
child's college education, your key parameters are historical: his/her GPA,
standardized test scores, field(s) of interest, aptitude, etc. While you fully
expect him/her to graduate, you would love to have a sense of what the
employment opportunities and earnings potential are over a certain time
horizon. This is where SAP PA can fill the gap based on the data that
you provide. And when this information is available in a timely manner,
you can make sure that your child applies to the appropriate schools and
potentially chooses the right field(s) of study.

2.1 Introduction to SAP PA

SAP introduced version 1.0 to the market in Q2 of 2012. It is important to note that it was not referred to as *predictive analytics* but rather *predictive analysis* and it was different than the current application. Predictive analysis was an application meant for analysts and data scientists. Although there was some visual/graphical content in the application that simplified the heavy lifting, it was not an application that regular/casual business users could use to any degree of usefulness.

SAP Predictive Analytics was first released in 2015. The motivation for building this product was twofold for regular business users (not just data scientists).

1. The ability to use it in a meaningful way, given that the marketplace was already being dominated by such applications.

2. The ability to transform and enrich a data set in an easy manner before being fed to the predictive algorithms. It is worthwhile to note that prior to SAP PA, this was being done by writing scripts/code. This made the transformation/enrichment of data a highly technical activity. Also, it was not transparent and was prone to errors.

So, SAP PA combined the original application, predictive analysis, with an application called Infinite Insight to deliver SAP PA.

So what is Infinite Insight? It is the flagship application from KXEN, a company SAP acquired in 2013. Infinite Insight takes away a lot of the heavy lifting that data scientists were best suited to do in the past and pushed this to the predictive engine. It helps the analysts do what they are supposed to do best: analyze, and not worry about preparing and modeling the data.

Back to SAP PA. The combination of these two products ensures that it caters to both major constituencies: data scientists and regular business users. You will have the option to use whichever embedded product best suits your needs and capabilities. The erstwhile predictive analysis component shows up as Expert Analytics and the incorporated Infinite Insight component appears as Automated Analytics. You might ask this: what are the similarities and differences? The answer to this question will unfold as I get into the details in subsequent chapters, but there are some similarities (more in the nature of functional overlaps) and some differences. You do not face a binary choice—you can use both flavors if you so desire.

2.2   History and evolution of SAP PA

Terms and phrases, such as machine learning, data mining, and artificial intelligence, among others, have caught the public imagination for many years and are currently part of the lexicon of the knowledge economy. You won't be surprised to learn (if you were not already aware) that predictive analysis embodies the features of each of these terms and sometimes is used in an interchangeable manner.

As briefly mentioned in Section 2.1, the SAP PA of today is a combination of two products:

1.   SAP Infinite Insight

2.   The original SAP Predictive Analytics

To distinguish Automated Analytics from the traditional SAP PA, the traditional application was renamed Expert Analytics. As the name might suggest, this application is a good fit for the data scientist and the statistically-savvy analyst. SAP PA, during its earliest releases, was an application that was best utilized by data scientists. It had a modest scope and there did not seem to be any illusions about what constituency the application would serve: the user interfaces were not friendly from a business user standpoint and analytics capabilities were rather limited. But it certainly was a starting point in addressing the need for SAP customers to more productively harness all the transaction data that was sitting in the SAP systems (and not just ERP but BW, CRM, and SRM systems). Wait! You might say. Why can't we use a data mining application like the Analysis Process Designer (APD) in SAP BW?

What is APD?

 APD is an integrated development environment fully built and incorporated into SAP BW that enables mining of data that is ingested into a business warehouse. It provides you with a set of transformation functions including logical ones (such as joining) and data mining ones (such as clustering and association analysis). APD allows you to push the output of these transformations to a selection of targets. Figure 2.1 displays the core components of APD.

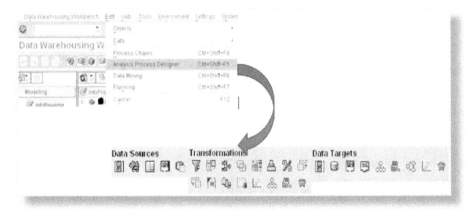

Figure 2.1: Core components of APD

Here are a variety of reasons you can't use APD in SAP BW:

▶ To use APD, you need to have SAP BW installed and operational in your enterprise. Operational means that relevant data must be flowing into your SAP BW environment so that you can use APD to mine the data.

▶ APD is not very robust when it comes to predictive capabilities. Compared to any true data mining application, APD would not be ranked too high. In other words, its true predictive capabilities are limited. Note that data mining and predictive analytics are not synonymous and APD is a good data mining application.

▶ A corollary to the previous bullet is that APD has a limited number of true "predictive" algorithms.

▶ Because it is a component of the SAP BW Administrator Workbench, it is tightly integrated with SAP BW. So if you are a user that does not have access and/or authorizations to an SAP BW system, you will not be able to use it.

▶ If you do not have at least basic SAP BW (technical) skills and a familiarity of SAP BW technical objects, you might struggle to be productive.

2.3 SAP PA architecture and technical components

There are two kinds of SAP PA deployments to choose from: desktop and enterprise.

2.3.1 SAP PA desktop

SAP PA desktop is the simplest type of deployment because you can download the necessary files and install it on your machine and can be up and running in a matter of minutes. The architecture consists of two components. The first is the analytics component, which itself consists of two sub-components: Expert Analytics and Automated Analytics (see Figure 2.2).

Figure 2.2: SAP Predictive Analytics main page

The second component is the source from which SAP PA pulls data from. Expert Analytics provides flexibility for you to connect with data from both flat files and tabular (RDBMS) databases, including SAP HANA. You can also connect to BusinessObjects (BO) universes. Automated Analytics is less versatile and only allows you to connect with data in SAS and SPSS

23

files, flat files in your local environment, or open database connectivity (ODBC) connections to select databases.

2.4   SAP PA with SAP HANA

Although SAP PA works as a standalone application, it can also leverage SAP HANA. Figure 2.3 shows how the SAP PA application and other tools and applications interact with the SAP HANA platform.

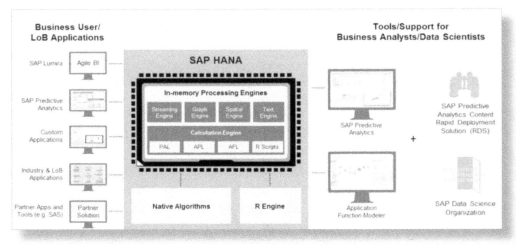

Figure 2.3: SAP PA integrated in SAP HANA

Data can be ingested into the SAP HANA platform from a multitude of applications, including SAP PA and other SAP applications such as SAP Lumira, a variety of custom applications, and partner applications such as SAS. SAP HANA's processing engine contains multiple libraries and scripts (PAL, APL, AFL, and R scripts) that SAP PA models can invoke. Since the processing of this data happens in-memory, you can take full advantage of the speed of the SAP HANA platform. The enriched data is now available for consumption and additional analysis in SAP PA.

Next up is a look at each of the processing components in SAP HANA relevant to SAP PA.

2.4.1 Predictive analytical library (PAL)

The predictive analytical library (PAL) is a library of advanced predictive functions built entirely using C++. As shown in Figure 2.3, PAL is embedded in the SAP HANA platform. Additionally, it is also available in the SAP Cloud Platform (SCP). PAL can be considered to be part of the application function library (AFL).

PAL prerequisite

 To utilize PAL functions, you need to be on SAP HANA 2.0.

Why do you need PAL? It is a combination of reasons. First, PAL is a compilation of sophisticated, comprehensive, and complex algorithms that covers a gamut of machine learning and data mining needs. It is quite possible to create one or more of these, but it is far more convenient and effortless to utilize a library of proven functions. I would like to qualify how possible it is for you to build your own function/script. It would actually pose quite a technical challenge, thus making the usage of PAL almost a no-brainer. Second, it is a truly powerful and speedy engine that can do real-time SAP PA. In many scenarios, organizations do not have the luxury of doing a data ETL to another system/machine and then running such algorithms. SAP HANA is that engine. So, by using PAL, you are outsourcing your SAP PA effort, complexity, and speed to software and hardware that are better equipped to handle these and provide you with minimal fuss for what you need most: the outputs.

How to use PAL?

 For the data scientist and the avid programmer: you can invoke PAL algorithms from within SQLScript code. This code will act as a *wrapper* to your PAL algorithm. Alternatively, you can directly call a PAL algorithm from a SQLScript procedure. SQLScript is the SAP HANA-based SQL and is enhanced to enable developers to realize complex application logic and embed the logic within database procedures.

The following is a list of function categories and algorithms available within PAL:

- ▶ Classification
- ▶ Clustering
- ▶ Regression
- ▶ Association
- ▶ Statistical
- ▶ Preprocessing
- ▶ Time series
- ▶ Social network analysis
- ▶ Others: such as ABC analysis and weighted table

Each of these categories has multiple algorithms. For details on these, please browse SAP documentation on the SAP Help website at: *https:// help.sap.com/viewer/2cfbc5cf2bc14f028cfbe2a2bba60a50/2.0.03/en-US/c9e eed704f3f4ec39441434db8a874ad.html*

2.4.2 Application function library (AFL)

PAL is a component of the application function library (AFL). AFL, as the name suggests, is a large library that contains functions. It organizes its content in folder-like archives with each folder representing a functional area. PAL contains the library of predictive algorithms.

2.4.3 SAP HANA automated predictive library (APL)

SAP's help website describes APL as a library that lets you use the data mining capabilities of the SAP Predictive Analytics automated analytics engine on your customer data sets stored in SAP HANA. It is a component of the AFL and therefore is a set of predictive functions. Like PAL, APL algorithms/functions are built in C++.

APL prerequisite

You need to be on SAP HANA SPS10 or higher to use APL.

One of the first questions you might ask is how APL is different from PAL.

▶ PAL enables you to utilize complex and sophisticated predictive needs while APL has simpler and more general-purpose data mining functions.

▶ PAL is for data scientists; APL can be used by non-technical users.

▶ APL operates in a black box manner or simply in a *feed the beast* manner. You feed data to APL and APL applies the algorithm(s) and provides you with the outputs.

2.5 SAP PA in SAP's BI roadmap

2.5.1 SAP's third quarter (2017) roadmap for SAP PA

The SAP PA roadmap that SAP published in the third quarter of 2017 and shown in Figure 2.4 firmly places SAP PA as the engine for machine learning.

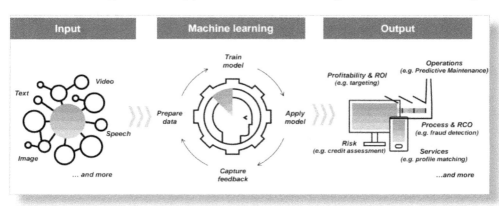

Figure 2.4: SAP PA roadmap

27

Simply put, you can pump all kinds of structured and non-structured data into this engine. After applying its models and running the algorithms, the output it provides helps enterprises make smarter decisions for the future.

This roadmap identifies the following as the core competencies of SAP PA:

▶ Prepare data for machine learning process

▶ Build predictive models in a rapid manner by using automation heavily for identifying both cause and effect, simulations of models, etc.

▶ Build complex predictive pipelines by utilizing existing assets such as the PAL, APL, unified demand forecast (UDF), and thousands of R functions and libraries

▶ Produce link analysis and recommendation models by identifying the causation links and their drivers to make appropriate recommendations

▶ Utilize in-database scoring capabilities by providing scoring through using interfaces to applications (Java, SQL, etc.)

▶ Automate predictive models lifecycle management by managing, scheduling, adjusting, and monitoring end-to-end predictive models in parallel

2.5.2   SAP's first quarter (2018) roadmap for SAP PA

All SAP investments 2018 and onwards for predictive analytics will be funneled to SAP Analytics Cloud (SAC). This is directly from the SAP roadmap shown in the SAP roadmap statement below.

> From Q1 2018 all net-new SAP Predictive Analytics development is being redirected into **SAP Analytics Cloud.** SAP is building a simple and compelling user experience for predictive workflows in SAP Analytics Cloud that will complement and enhance existing business intelligence and planning capabilities. The focus is to provide **self-service data science** capabilities including support for data ingestion, model creation, and model management.
>
> **SAP Predictive Analytics** is a robust and mature on-premise solution that will continue to be available for customers to purchase and will be maintained and supported until at least December 31, 2022. SAP Predictive Analytics continues to benefit from investment in related innovations such as the **SAP Predictive Analytics integrator** that allows customers to build predictive models and embed them directly into SAP solutions such as SAP S/4HANA. SAP plans to make SAP Predictive Analytics part of the cloud extension policy to enable partial terminations of on-premise maintenance when combined with a new contract for SAP Analytics Cloud.

There is a lot of information embedded into these two bullets. The good news is that if you have invested in SAP PA or plan on investing in SAP PA, this will not be a lost cause. I highly recommend leveraging the predictive capabilities in the SAP HANA platform in conjunction with SAP PA. Meanwhile, SAP is heavily ramping up on SAP Analytics Cloud (SAC) as its premier application for both prescriptive and predictive analytics. It is to be noted that SAC has had embedded predictive capabilities from its earliest days, although these were lightweight in comparison to a pure predictive product like SAP PA. But as of Q1 2018, SAP started significantly augmenting the predictive capabilities of SAC.

2.6   Installation

SAP PA comes in two separate flavors:

1. **Desktop version**: As the name suggests, this version is meant for the individual user and is an independent application that can be downloaded from SAP's software download site.

2. **Enterprise version**: This is a three-tier client-server edition that needs to be installed on a server running the Microsoft or Linux operating system. There is a client-side installation for every machine that needs to connect to the back end.

SAP PA desktop version

 This book is focused on the desktop version of SAP PA. The installation steps below are for the desktop version.

---

3. Once you are licensed to download it, navigate to *https://launchpad. support.sap.com/#/softwarecenter*. You will see the (landing) screen, as shown in Figure 2.5.

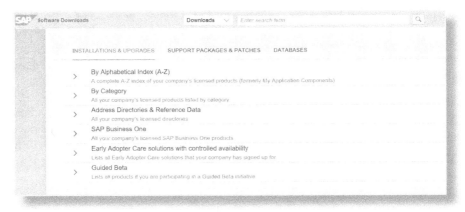

Figure 2.5: SAP software download center

Although you can search for the SAP PA application in the search box next to DOWNLOADS, you might get overwhelmed with all the hits. I recommend going in a structured manner:

▶ Click the arrow to the left of BY CATEGORY to view content. The (partial) list appears, as shown in Figure 2.6.

Figure 2.6: Downloads by category

▶ Now click ANALYTICS SOLUTIONS to move to the screen that contains all the analytics/BI solutions. There are quite a few, so scroll down until you see PREDICTIVE ANALYTICS. A partial screenshot is shown in Figure 2.7.

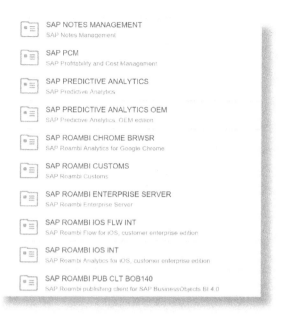

Figure 2.7: SAP PA download junction

▶ Now click SAP PREDICTIVE ANALYTICS to go to the page (currently) showing two release tracks available for download. This is shown in Figure 2.8.

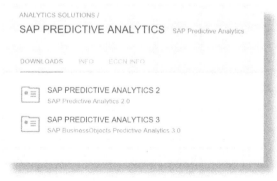

Figure 2.8: SAP PA release tracks for downloading

▶ Presumably, you will be interested in the latest version (i.e. the 3.x version). Click the appropriate track to go to another screen that shows you two options. See Figure 2.9.

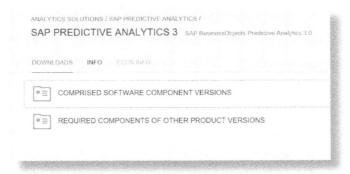

Figure 2.9: SAP PA download options

▶ At this point in time, only pay attention to the option, COMPRISED SOFTWARE COMPONENT VERSIONS. The wording is a little awkward, but what it essentially means is that this option contains all the constituent files needed to run SAP PA. Once you click this option, the next screen, as shown in Figure 2.10, will list the various files available for downloading and installation.

Figure 2.10: Download options for individual SAP PA components

▶ Initially, you might be overwhelmed with the various download op-tions. Suffice it to say the version to download at the outset as an individual user is the PREDICTIVE ANALYTICS DESKTOP 3 ver-sion. Of course you are welcome to browse the contents of each of these download libraries at any time.

Other downloadable items

 The other libraries contain files that either are not relevant, or require an advanced understanding of the product. As an example, SAP PA comes with a library of functions encapsulated in APL. This is of value to a data scientist, but if you are new to SAP PA or are a casual user, you can be productive without this library.

When you click SAP PREDICTIVE ANALYTICS DESKTOP 3, you should see a screen similar to what is shown in Figure 2.11.

PREDICTIVE ANALYTICS DESKTOP 3

DOWNLOADS   INFO   EULA INFO

Multispanning: Packages that are larger than 4 GB will be packed in an archive, which is split into 4 GB parts. All archives need to be downloaded and unpacked. For more details on multispanning and how to extract the multi-part .exe archive on UNIX See SAP Note 886535.

Items Available to Download (4)   WINDOWS ON X64 64BIT

Selected items (0)

Name	Patch Level	File Type	File Size	Release Date	Change Date	Related Info
PADESKTOP3003P_2-70001855.EXE						
Patch 2 for SAP Predictive Analytics DESKTOP 3.3	2	EXE	626926 KB	09.03.2018	09.03.2018	
PADESKTOP3002P_1-70001855.EXE						
Patch 1 for PREDICTIVE ANALYTICS DESKTOP 3.2	1		606926 KB	11.08.2017	11.08.2017	
PADESKTOP3002_0-70001855.EXE						
PREDICTIVE ANALYTICS DESKTOP 3.2	0		606978 KB	11.08.2017	11.08.2017	
PADESKTOP3001P_3-70001855.EXE						
Patch 3 for PREDICTIVE ANALYTICS DESKTOP 3.1	3	EXE	721160 KB	26.04.2017	26.04.2017	

(*) for validation only

Figure 2.11: SAP PA executables for downloading

On this screen, you select the executable for the latest version of SAP PA that's generally available (3.2 in our case) and then download and install on your machine.

3 Core components and units

In the previous chapter, I introduced you to the key elements of SAP PA, including its history, evolution, high-level architecture, the key components, where and how SAP PA fits into SAP's analytics/BI road-map, and the steps you need to carry out to successfully install SAP PA.

It is now time to go into the details of each of the components and understand how they work.

3.1 Data manager

The data manager enables you to prepare and manage your data so that it is ready for consumption by SAP PA algorithms for additional processing. When you select DATA MANAGER from the main menu, the screen will be similar to what is shown in Figure 3.1.

Welcome to

SAP Predictive Analytics®

Data Manager

Create or Edit Analytic Data
Create a Data Manipulation
Load an Existing Data Manipulation
Perform an Event Log Aggregation
Perform a Sequence Analysis
Perform a Text Analysis

Figure 3.1: Data manager landing page

This page is your entry point to the data manager application. Let's look at the options available.

▶ **Create or edit analytic data**—In this step you create/acquire and/or edit a data set. You have the option of storing the metadata in

the same place as your data (default option) or specifying a separate location. See Figure 3.2.

Figure 3.2: Connecting to data manager

Please note that you will need to create an ODBC connection to the metadata repository of your choice that contains your metadata. It is highly
likely that you will need to enter your credentials to gain access before you
can edit the data.

▶ **Create a data manipulation**—In this step, you can modify or enhance an existing data set to create a data manipulation. As in the
  previous step, you will need to connect to a metadata repository
  that sits atop the database you want to connect to. Since this database is likely to be password-protected, you will need to provide
  your user credentials to connect. Once you successfully connect,
  you can use the analytical data set editor to carry out your data
  modifications and enhancements.

▶ **Load an existing data manipulation**—In this step, you load the
  data manipulation you created in the previous step. In this activity,
  you can also delete an existing manipulation. When you click LOAD
  AN EXISTING DATA MANIPULATION, the application takes you to a
  new screen, as shown in Figure 3.3.

Figure 3.3: Opening an existing data set

Here, you will need to identify the datatype and the corresponding database. You will then have to provide your credentials to connect to the database. Once you do so, all the data manipulations you have created so far will be visible. You can either open a data manipulation or delete it.

▶ **Perform an event log aggregation**—In this activity, you will be merging two data sets aggregated by time dimensions. So it is mandatory to have at least one time dimension in each of your data sets. This aggregated data can then be processed with a classification or a clustering model.

▶ **Perform a sequence analysis**—This is an operation applied to your data set prior to running an SAP PA algorithm. It arranges the data into a sequence of events that transition one event to another. Sequence analysis is typically used with high-volume web-based customer transactions data.

▶ **Perform a text analysis**—This is a valuable capability that allows you to mine your data set and do a text analysis to detect trends and patterns. The outcome of a text analysis is useful metrics for the text variables that you have identified. The text analysis algorithms identify the important words based on how relevant they match your need.

> **Tip**
>
> A question that comes up in this area is: What if the text is some language other than English? The good news is that SAP PA supports multiple languages.

3.2 Performing an event log aggregation

Now go through the steps of creating an event log aggregation. When you click on PERFORM AN EVENT LOG AGGREGATION as shown in Figure 3.1 , you go to the screen to choose the modeling feature/algorithm to apply to your data set. See Figure 3.4.

Figure 3.4: Selecting a modeling algorithm

There are three options available:

1. **Add a Classification/Regression**: The application creates a classification/regression atop an aggregation table.

2. **Add a Clustering**: The application creates a clustering model atop an aggregation table.

3. **Standalone Data Transformation**: The application creates an aggregation table. In effect, this is the first step in the previous two options. The application must generate the aggregation table before you do any modeling.

Try out the second option. When you click ADD A CLUSTERING, you are taken to a new screen, as shown in Figure 3.5.

Figure 3.5: Preparing to add a data set

The folder path and data set need to be entered. I will be using a retail data set that I have saved on the local drive of my machine. Click NEXT. See Figure 3.6

Figure 3.6: Application after adding data set

The application will prompt you to analyze the metadata. In a majority of situations, we tend to do a perfunctory browse of the metadata and move on. However in this situation, it is important to carefully analyze the data fields. Note that you must have at least one date field in each of your data sets. Let's look at the metadata to see if that is the case. See Figure 3.7.

Figure 3.7: Browsing the metadata of added data set

The DATE line in Figure 3.7 is highlighted because it currently shows DATE-TIME format. To change the format, select DATE from the drop-down menu, then click NEXT. See Figure 3.8.

SAP Predictive Analytics® (Data Manager) - New Model with Event Log Aggregation

File   Help

Events Data Source

Data Type: Excel 2007 Workbook   ∨

Folder: |

Events:

Figure 3.8: Incorporating events data source

Enter the folder path for the retail data set and specify the file name in the EVENTS box. Click NEXT. See Figure 3.9.

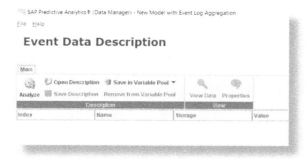

Figure 3.9: Getting ready to preview your data

A message appears to remind you to analyze the data before executing the next step. Once you analyze the data, and assuming you are satisfied with what you see, click NEXT. See Figure 3.10.

Figure 3.10: Configuring event logging

Notice reference to two data sets: the EVENT DATA SET and the REFERENCE DATA SET. As a reminder, in our example, we are using the same data set for both sets. The COLUMNS FOR JOINS is an important driver for event logging. It is that common property that lets you combine the two data sets. Analyze your data set carefully and then make your decision.

Column combinations

 You can only combine columns whose data types are *nominal*. You cannot combine any other data types. In case you have inadvertently or otherwise selected a *continuous* data type, click PREVIOUS to make sure you select columns that are nominal.

Select CITY and COUNTRY as the join columns; both of them are of type nominal. Since one field was set to be of DATE type, the data manager automatically defaults in this field as the EVENT DATE COLUMN.

Now look at STORAGE TYPE. This becomes an important consideration when you are dealing with large volumes of data. (We are dealing with a small sample data set, so the selection of the storage type will not matter much). If you select the ON DISK option, the generated data will be stored on your machine's hard disk. It is slower than the other option of storing your data in your machine's main memory, but it can handle larger volumes. If you prefer to save the data to memory, the trade-off for the speedy access is the inability to store large volumes.

Choose appropriate storage mode

 Event logging creates multiple new columns that are based on the existing data sets and thus a whole lot of additional content. Therefore, it is important to choose the storage mode to prevent the application from crashing.

Last, and the least important, is the VARIABLE PREFIX. The default setting is *el* for all variables. I cannot think of any compelling reason to change this, but in case there is one, the option for you to do so is available.

It's time for the next step. Click NEXT. The resulting (partial) screen is shown in Figure 3.11. At the top of the screen, there are two settings: SIMPLE CONFIGURATION and ADVANCED CONFIGURATION. The default is simple configuration. You can configure your aggregates, periods, and filters here. Configuring your filter settings is an optional activity.

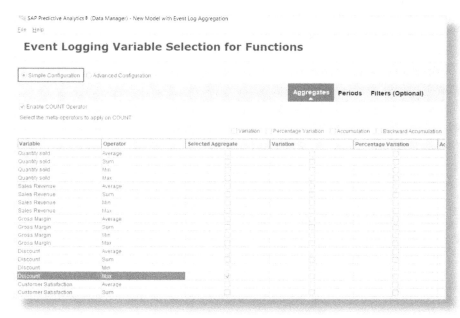

Figure 3.11: Simple and advanced configurations

3.3 Performing a text analysis

Let's see it in action. When you click PERFORM A TEXT ANALYSIS, it takes you to the screen shown in Figure 3.12.

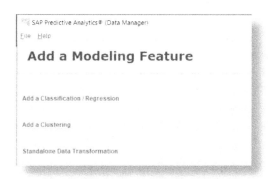

Figure 3.12: Text analysis options

Here you have three options: ADD A CLASSIFICATION/REGRESSION, ADD A CLUSTE-RING, and STANDALONE DATA TRANSFORMATION. Let's add a classification/regression because this is the easiest one to understand. Clicking this option takes us to the screen shown in Figure 3.13.

Figure 3.13: Providing file name and path for your data set

On this screen, select the option EXCEL 2007 WORKBOOK from the DATA TYPE drop-down. Specify the folder and the file: use the retail data set. Click the NEXT button. See Figure 3.14.

Figure 3.14: Getting ready to analyze your metadata

Analyze the data set. When you click ANALYZE, you are taken to the next screen which has a message at the bottom. At least one of the variables in your data set must be set to TEXTUAL. This is shown in Figure 3.15.

Figure 3.15: Adjusting data type in metadata preview

Why is it mandatory to set at least one field as a text field?

SAP PA text analysis algorithms need text fields to perform text analysis. They are not designed to work on any other data type.

Now click NEXT. See Figure 3.16. This is an important screen, so take a long look at it.

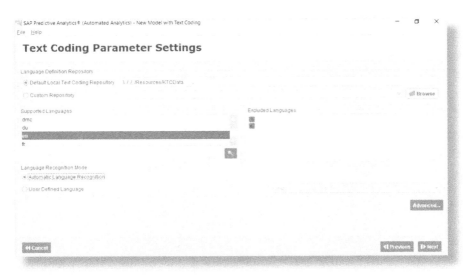

Figure 3.16: Maintaining settings for text coding

The first parameter, the DEFAULT TEXT CODING REPOSITORY, contains all the relevant language files. You can specify a custom repository. In the SUPPORTED LANGUAGES box, scroll down to see the list of available languages for the text analysis. You can choose from either AUTOMATIC LANGUAGE RECOGNITION mode or USER DEFINED LANGUAGE mode. You can also exclude languages to ensure that the analyisis algorithms only take into account the languages you include.

Text analysis in a single language

In an increasingly globalized world, it is fairly common for individuals, if not organizations, to communicate in multiple languages. Text analysis that is done in a single language is likely to be less effective.

You can customize the application for some advanced activities by clicking
ADVANCED. See Figure 3.17.

Figure 3.17: Maintaining advanced text coding parameters

On this screen, you can specify any words you want analyzed. Stop words, such as prepositions or articles, do not aid or enhance your analysis. You can create a list of stop words and save it to a file. You can also load a stop-word list that you may have previously created, or that is available. Once that list is created or loaded, you can have specific stop words excluded by highlighting that word and clicking the "-" button located at the bottom of that section.

Once you have created your list or determined you don't have any stop words, click PREVIOUS to return to the prior screen. Click NEXT to move to the screen where you set text coding parameters. This is shown in Figure 3.18.

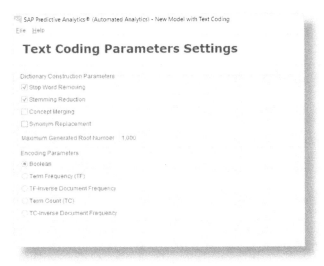

Figure 3.18: Setting specific text coding parameters

I will skip explanation of these parameters because as a relatively new user of SAP PA, you are highly unlikely to be doing any configuration for text coding. It is sufficient for you to be familiar with the screen. You can safely click the NEXT button to go to the screen shown in Figure 3.19 to view the results.

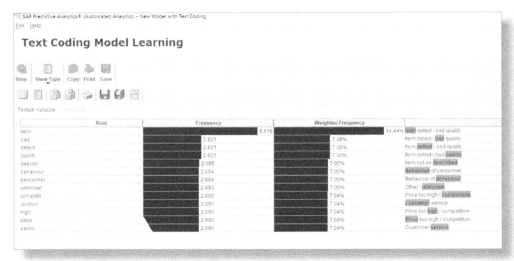

Figure 3.19: Results of model learning

The text analysis has found that the word *item* was referenced the most. That should not come as a surprise since the data set contained retail data. What should raise your eyebrows is that the word *bad* appeared as many times as it did and also in conjunction with *quality*. When you combine the frequency of occurrences of *bad quality* with *item defect*, we find a total of 14.76% of the items in the data set received customer feedback of *item defect/bad quality*.

3.4   Automated analytics

Automated analytics consists of three components: MODELER, SOCIAL, and RECOMMENDATION. Using these components, you are able to traverse the entire predictive analytics spectrum, from modeling with your data set (i.e applying various modeling techniques), to creating social network analysis, to obtaining recommendations based on social network analysis. Let's go into the details of each of these components.

3.4.1   Modeler

The modeler allows you to choose from a variety of techniques to build predictive models based on the data set you provide. You can access the modeler by clicking MODELER which appears when you expand the AUTO-MATED ANALYTICS node. See Figure 3.20.

Figure 3.20: Options in SAP PA modeler

1. Classification/regression model

Before I illustrate classification/regression functionality in SAP PA, let me explain the concepts of classification and regression in simple terms. It is important to have a good grasp of these concepts since they are not only of importance to data mining and predictive analytics but also are core concepts in machine learning.

Classification is a technique where the available data set is placed/classified into different groups. It is used to answer questions that have a numeric response. Binary classification is used when you are seeking *yes* or *no* answers to your question/prediction. A good example of this is, "Should I target customer X with product Y?" or "Will employee X leave company Y in 2020?" The other type of classification is multi-label classification where there are two or more possibilities. It is popularly used in areas such as text analysis.

Regression has a key difference with classification. Regression outcomes are continuous values. When a regression algorithm is applied to a data set, the output can be represented as a continuous variable and will not assume discrete values. Linear regression is a popular SAP PA technique that has its origins in statistical analysis and its results are fairly simple to comprehend. When the time dimension is one of the input variables, time-series forecasting is a specific use case of regression. I will dive deeper into time-series forecasting in Chapter 4.

Clicking the first option CREATE A CLASSIFICATION/REGRESSION MODEL shown in Figure 3.20 takes you to the screen shown in Figure 3.21.

Figure 3.21: Selecting a data source

Let's pick a sample SAP data set that contains (fictitious) data on the best-run retail corporations, and then click NEXT. See Figure 3.22.

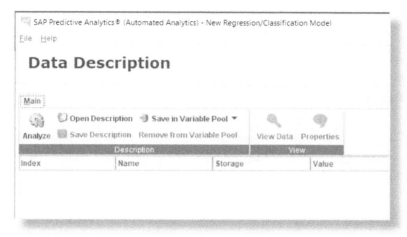

Figure 3.22: Getting ready to analyze metadata

You can do an analysis of your metadata here by clicking the ANALYZE button.

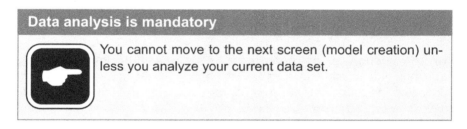

The generated metadata is shown in Figure 3.23.

51

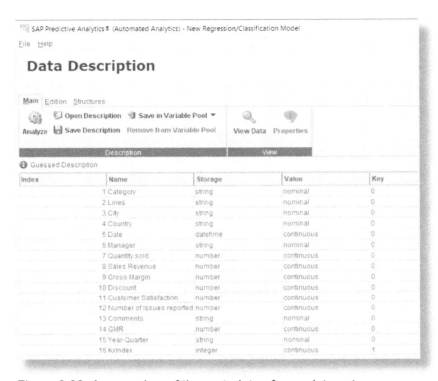

Figure 3.23: An overview of the metadata of your data set

On this screen you can do other things such as add or remove a struc-
ture; populate missing data; and make changes to the metadata, including
changing the data type, etc. You can also view the data in a tabular, statistical, or graph option. Click the VIEW DATA button to do this. The result is
shown in Figure 3.24.

Figure 3.24: Preparing input and output variables

To see the statistical information pertaining to this data set instead, click the STATISTICS button. See Figure 3.25.

Figure 3.25: Setting parameters for computing statistics

Click the COMPUTE STATISTICS OVER THE WHOLE DATA SET button. Figure 3.26 displays the resulting (partial) screenshot after you select the CATEGORY FREQUENCIES option.

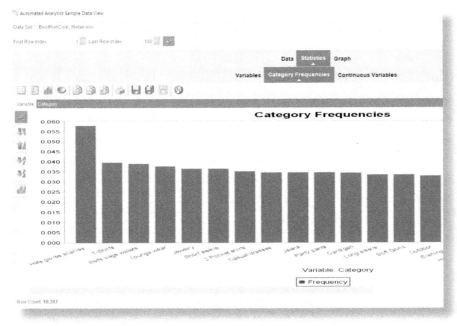

Figure 3.26: Category frequencies

Category frequencies displays the frequency of occurrence of each category. I use the word category in a generic sense. What I really mean is that the frequency of occurrence of each input variable/field/column is displayed here. It just so happens that the first field is actually named CATEGORY.

Now change the category variable to CITY by clicking the variable drop-down, as shown in Figure 3.26. A partial screenshot of the output is shown in Figure 3.27.

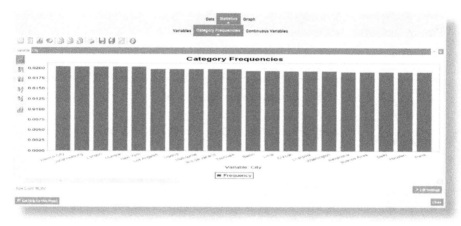

Figure 3.27: Category frequencies by city

For measures of central tendency, click CONTINUOUS VARIABLES, as shown in Figure 3.26. The statistical information provides you with data that gives you metrics around the range of the data set for each of the columns and their central tendency manifested in the mean and standard deviation. This is shown in Figure 3.28.

Obviously, the statistical summary applies only to the numeric data in the data set. You get a fair idea of your data set. This is difficult to obtain without some kind of an aggregation tool like SAP PA. So, for example, we now know that the data spans three calendar years. You can click the CLOSE button to return to the DATA DESCRIPTION screen. You will notice the CUTTING STRATEGY button.

Figure 3.28: Statistical summary of data set

Cutting strategy

 So, what exactly is a cutting strategy? Cutting strategy splits your input data set into two or three subsets to improve the accuracy of the predictions. It builds an estimation subset for training the models and a validation subset for consistency. It may create a third data set (known as test subset) for calculating the final model quality indicator.

Look at the various cutting strategy options available for selection. Click CUTTING STRATEGY, as shown in Figure 3.21, and then do a drop-down on the PREDEFINED field. This is shown in Figure 3.29.

Figure 3.29: Options for cutting strategy

56

RANDOM WITHOUT TEST is the default. At this stage of your understanding of SAP PA, it is fine to stick to the default. This means that all you need to do is click OK at the bottom of the screen to move to the next screen. (A discussion on each of these options is beyond the scope of this book, but you are encouraged to try each one.)

Now, click NEXT. See Figure 3.30.

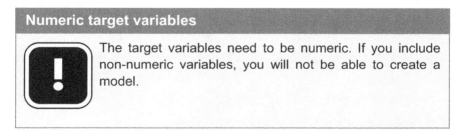

Figure 3.30: Identify target and excluded variables

To keep things uncomplicated at this early stage, select QUANTITY SOLD as the target variable. As might be obvious, moving variables from one panel to another is a simple matter of highlighting that particular field and clicking the appropriate arrow. I would like to retain all the input variables as contributing variables. The application excludes by default the KRINDEX variable.

Numeric target variables

! The target variables need to be numeric. If you include non-numeric variables, you will not be able to create a model.

57

Let's move forward. Click NEXT. See Figure 3.31.

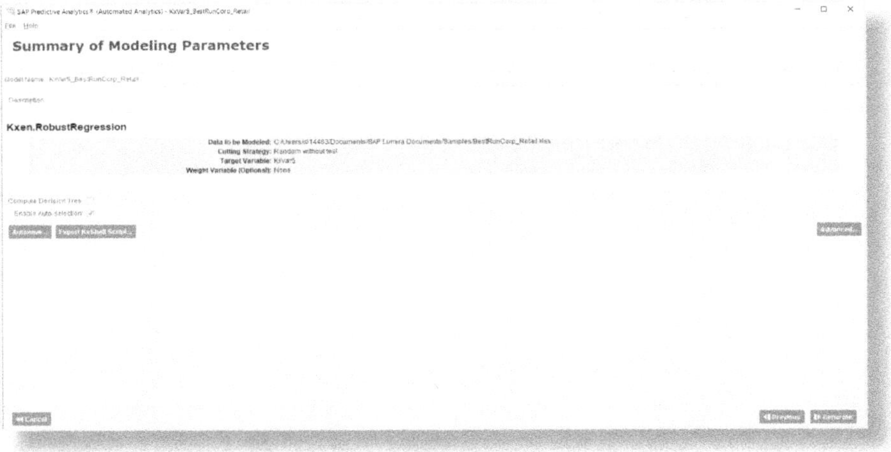

Figure 3.31: Summary of modeling variables

Make sure you have the two checkboxes: COMPUTE DECISION TREE and ENAB-
LE AUTO-SELCTION selected as shown. You can change the model name to
something that is appropriate and also provide a description. If you are
curious about what is in the ADVANCED tab, click it. You will see a screen
similar to the one shown in Figure 3.32.

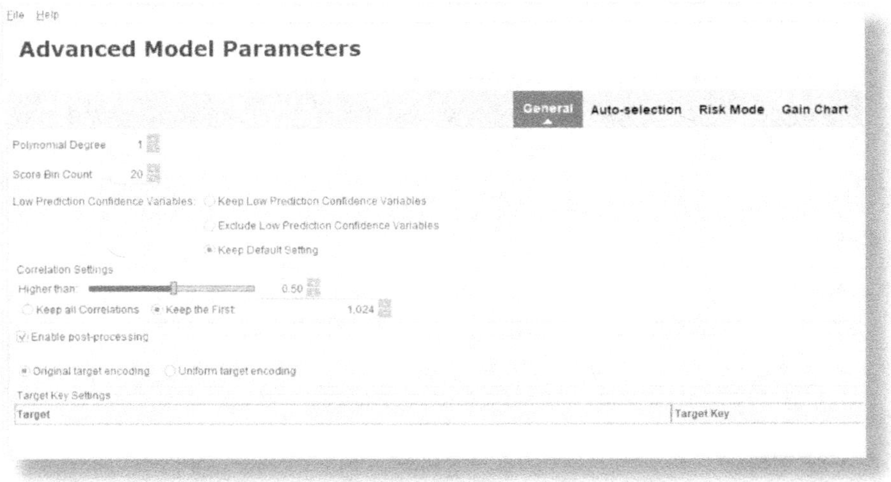

Figure 3.32: Additional (advanced) parameters

I would highly recommend that you stick to the defaults and click PREVIOUS once you have absorbed the information displayed in the various tabs of this screen. Click GENERATE, as shown in Figure 3.31. SAP PA will take some time to build the training model. How much time it takes depends on the size and complexity of your data set as well as the kind of cutting strategy you have selected. Upon completion, you will be provided an overview of the training model, as shown in Figure 3.33.

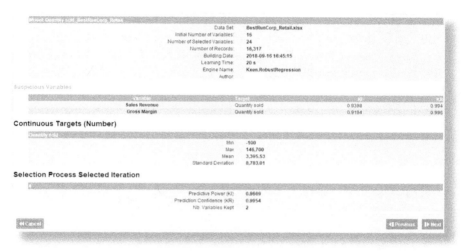

Figure 3.33: Overview of training model

Take a close look at this results screen. It contains all relevant information with respect to your data set and the various variables. Of particular relevance and importance are the *suspicious variables*. Why are sales revenue and gross margin flagged as suspicious? To understand that, let me explain two KPIs, namely the predictive power (KI) and predictive confidence (KR).

KI measures how closely your input variables contribute to the target variable. A very high percent (such as the one we obtained) informs us that there are one or more input variables that is/are very closely aligned with the target. Such variables are flagged as *suspicious*. In the example with our data set, the sales revenue and gross margin are too closely correlated to the quantity sold and thus increase the value of KI. So for better training models, we should exclude these two variables as input variables in the future. The rationale is simple: there is no point in including these since the behavior of these variables are almost perfectly in sync with the target

59

variable. KI can be 0, in which case the relationship is totally random but cannot be 1. The closer it is to 1, the less effective your training model is based on the existing combination of input and target variables.

KR indicates how accurate you can expect the application of this model to new data. It is a percent measure of the confidence and naturally the higher it is, the better. Our model has around a 99% KR which means that we can successfully apply this model to new data.

You can switch to an executive view of the model results by switching to EXECUTIVE REPORT in the REPORT TYPE drop-down. A partial screenshot of this is shown in Figure 3.34.

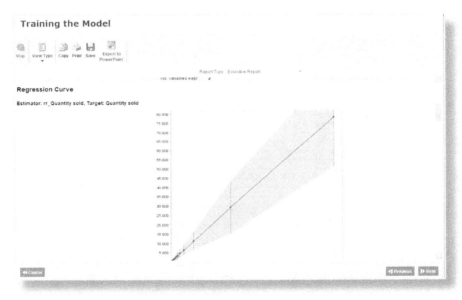

Figure 3.34: Executive view of model

There is a lot of information to be consumed in this view as you scroll down. You will see a lot of regression curves for your analysis. This will not be of much use because there are better analytical tools and capabilities lying ahead. So click NEXT. See Figure 3.35.

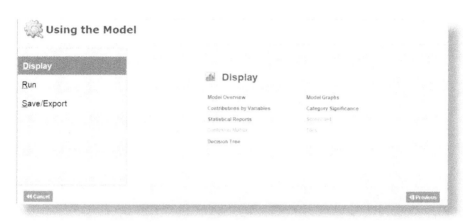

Figure 3.35: Utilizing training model

This screen shows many options to display and analyze the results from this model. The available options are hyperlinked.

Note that until now we have only prepared the model for an actual run. In simple terms, the application has learned some key facts from the data set and is now ready to apply these facts and lessons. Let's run the model by clicking RUN. See Figure 3.36.

Figure 3.36: Getting ready to run the model

Let's do a test run first. Click SIMULATION. See Figure 3.37.

61

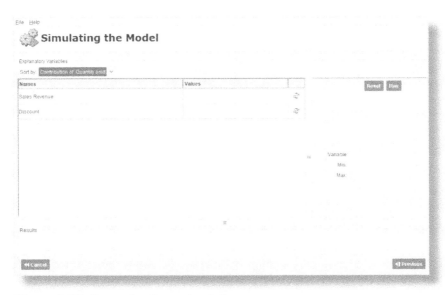

Figure 3.37: Preparing for a simulation run

Click RUN. It will generate results. This is shown in Figure 3.38.

Figure 3.38: Results of simulation

Click PREVIOUS to return to the previous screen (Figure 3.36). Click SELECT VARIABLE. See Figure 3.39.

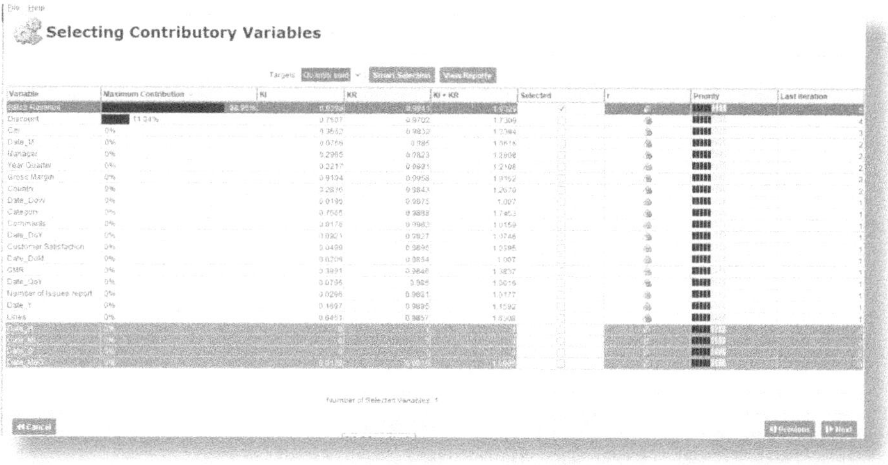

Figure 3.39: Selecting contributory variables

The algorithm has determined that sales revenue has the greatest contribution to the quantity sold (around 89%) followed by discount (around 11%). What may be surprising is that all other input variables seem to have no impact on the quantity sold. For a better quantitative understanding of the impact, look at the values of KI and KR for each of the variables. A column that is of interest is PRIORITY. When you mouse-over this column, the application will display the correlated input variable names and respective KIs.

Finally, it is time to apply the model. Click PREVIOUS, as shown in Figure 3.37. You will get the screen shown in Figure 3.38. Click APPLY MODEL and you will see the screen shown in Figure 3.40.

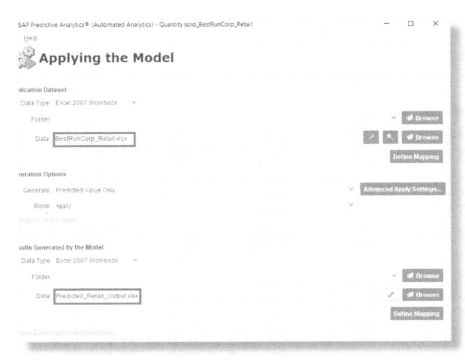

Figure 3.40: Applying model to existing data set

To apply the model, you need to provide the name and location of your data set. You can see the name of the data set outlined in red.

Applying models to data sets

 You can apply the model to another data set. In the previous activities, we trained the model using the training data set. The purpose of this is to make the model as smart as possible. This is the basic premise of machine learning in microcosm.

You also need to provide the name of the location/folder and file where the results should be saved. The name of the destination data set is outlined in red.

The parameters in the GENERATION OPTIONS panel have multiple options. At this stage of learning SAP PA, let's stay with the defaults, i.e. we want the model to generate predicted values only and APPLY as the mode. An area I would like to draw your attention to in Figure 3.40 is the DEFINE MAPPING button. Click this to move to the screen shown in Figure 3.41.

Figure 3.41: Mapping of fields between source and target data set

What is the signficance of this screen? In case you use a different data set with fields that are different from the training data set, you will need to map the new fields on this screen to those of the training data set so that the training model can be meaningfully applied to the new data set. You do not need to do anything right now because you are using the same data set. You can click the PREVIOUS button to return to the screen shown in Figure 3.37. You're ready to finally run the model. Click APPLY. You will see a screen similar to what is shown in Figure 3.39. If your model has been succesfully applied to the data set and it has run to completion, you will see a success message (see Figure 3.42).

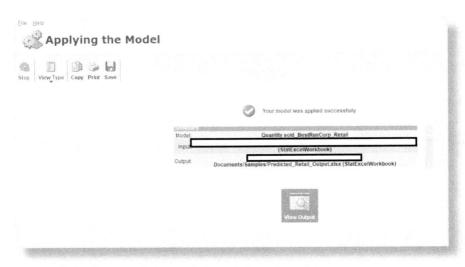

Figure 3.42: Successful completion status of model run

Click the VIEW OUTPUT button and it will take you through a set of screens that you'll recognize from the earlier training and simulation exercise. If you have the exact same data set (meaning that you have no additional records), the predictions should match those of the training data set. If you provide an augmented data set, you are likely to see different predictions because the training model will now be applied to an updated data set and the predictions will now be based on the lessons learned from the training data set that are then applied to the new data set. Regardless, you can explore the results by going through the various screens.

You will finally be taken to the screen shown in Figure 3.43.

The last thing to do is to save or export your model. The simplest thing to do at this stage is to save your model for future use by other users and analysts. Click the SAVE MODEL option. It takes you to the screen shown in Figure 3.44.

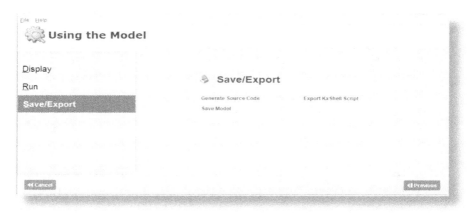

Figure 3.43: Preparing to save your model

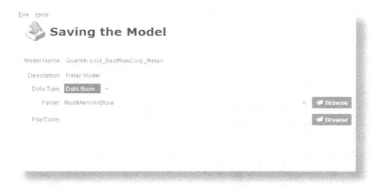

Figure 3.44: Saving the model

Give your model an appropriate technical name and description. In the DATA TYPE field, you have three options in the drop-down: DATABASE, TEXT FILE, and FLAT MEMORY. At this time, you shouldn't worry about what format this model is stored in. Select DATABASE. When you save the model, it will be available for selection when you want to do predictive analytics on additional data sets in the future.

2. Clustering

This is a data mining technique that goes hand in hand with regression. It organizes the data into groups called *clusters*. As such, you have a lot of the same features as with classification analysis. You will see a summary of the inputs and the outputs, the impact of each of the categories on the targets, graphs that visually convey the relationship between cause and effect, and so on. Unique to clustering is the ability to see clusters on a bar chart sorted by frequency, relative mean, or target mean.

When you click the link CREATE A CLUSTERING MODEL in the MODELER screen you will see the screen shown in Figure 3.45.

Figure 3.45: Identifying a data source for applying a clustering algorithm

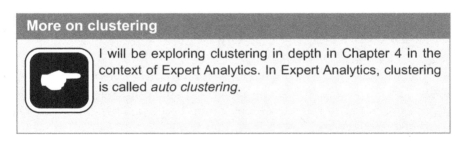

More on clustering

I will be exploring clustering in depth in Chapter 4 in the context of Expert Analytics. In Expert Analytics, clustering is called *auto clustering*.

The next set of actions is generally similar to those that you took for the classification/regression model.

3. Time-series analysis

A time-series algorithm helps you do trends and forecasts. It is a fairly common technique in data mining and predictive analytics. In SAP PA, to do a time-series analysis on your data set, the data set must have at least one date/time field such as year, month and year, or quarter and year, etc. The forecast is done for a target variable. This is a numeric variable such as sales, inflation, headcount, etc.

4. Association rules

Association rules go hand in hand with techniques such as classification, regression, clustering, and time-series analysis in terms of its popularity and importance in data mining and predictive analytics. In this technique, the algorithm detects hidden trends, patterns, and associations among variables in a data set. Extending this concept to machine learning, association rules train your model to learn such associations in your data set to make it smarter in detecting similar patterns in future data sets. A popular use case of association rules is *market basket analysis*.

What is market basket analysis?

 Market basket analysis is a data mining technique frequently employed in retailing. By analyzing the nature of customer purchases, retailers can position products more effectively. In a literal sense, your market basket contains certain combinations of items and such patterns are of tremendous value from a data mining and predictive analytics perspective.

5. Load a model

This is an activity in the modeler. It is not a data mining or SAP PA technique. Clicking this option displays the generic data set loading interface screen you have previously seen.

3.4.2 Social

In this hyperconnected world, the data explosion we are regularly dealing with is in a social context. When your Facebook friends "like" a picture or link you posted, it has to be viewed in the context of your Facebook network. When LinkedIn recommends individuals that you might want to connect with, your profile is being analyzed by LinkedIn's algorithms in a social context. So, this somewhat cryptically named function enables you to create and analyze these relationships in a graphical manner.

Let's look at the social nature of SAP PA by clicking the SOCIAL menu item, as shown in Figure 3.20. You will see a screen similar to what is shown in Figure 3.46.

Figure 3.46: Landing page for social analysis

Let's say we want to create a social network analysis. If you click the first link CREATE A SOCIAL NETWORK ANALYSIS, as shown in Figure 3.46 you will see the screen shown in Figure 3.47.

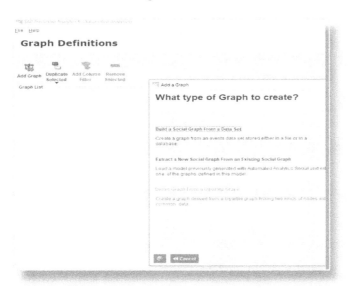

Figure 3.47: Graph options for social network analysis

To create a colocation analysis, click the second link CREATE A COLOCATION ANALYSIS, as shown in Figure 3.46. You will then see the screen displayed in Figure 3.48.

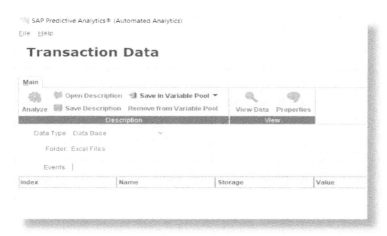

Figure 3.48: Supplying a data set and event data for colocation analysis

Now back to Figure 3.46. Click again on CREATE A SOCIAL NETWORK ANALYSIS and in the resulting screen click BUILD A SOCIAL GRAPH FROM A DATA SET. You will see the resulting screen shown in Figure 3.49.

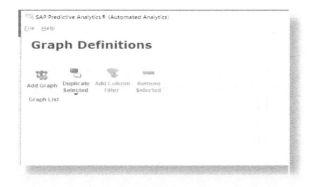

Figure 3.49: Getting ready to add a graph

Now click ADD GRAPH and you will see the screen shown in Figure 3.50.

Figure 3.50: Providing the necessary data

You need to identify the data set on which the social graph needs to be generated. Let's continue to use the retail data set. Once you provide that information, make sure to analyze the data set. Then click NEXT and the resulting screen, as shown in Figure 3.51, appears.

Let's look at the fields on this screen and understand what they mean and what you need to do with them. When you click DUPLICATE SELECTED, you can clone the currently selected graph. To filter your data set on one or more aspects, click ADD COLUMN FILTER.

Let's say you want to filter the data to contain records with the first four cities that appear in the data set in alphabetical order. Select CITY as the FILTERED COLUMN from the drop-down, select the ACCEPT radio button, and then click the binoculars button to select the cities you want added. Once you have highlighted the cities, transfer them to the filter and go back to the main graph creation screen, as shown in Figure 3.51.

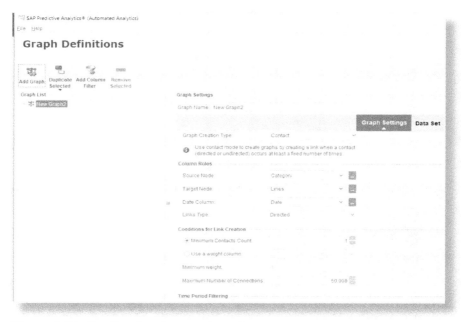

Figure 3.51: Configuring the graph settings

Let's look at each of the sections:

Graph creation type

There are five options to choose from.

1. **Contact** (default): The graph will contain only the links found a specified number of times.

2. **Transactions**: The graph will contain relationships between unrelated components/fields.

3. **Proximity**: This type of graph is used for geographical/locational analysis. As such, your data set must contain at least one geographical dimension.

4. **Nearest neighbors**: This advanced type of graph contains a specific number of nearest neighbors for each node. Nearest neighbors are determined by their relative distance, which must be specified in a separate column.

5. **Links only**: This simple network graph links values from the source columns to those of the target columns.

Column roles

1. **Source node**: Pick the field you want as your source (node) from the drop-down.

2. **Target node**: Pick the field you want as your target (node) from the drop-down.

Must have different source and target names

 If you have selected the same field as both the source and target node, the application will flag this as an error and you will need to change it. The source and the target nodes cannot be the same.

3. **Date columns**: If there is a date component in your data set, you can select an appropriate date field. It is not mandatory to do so. However, including a date dimension might help in filtering the data.

4. **Links type**: This field is relevant only for graph types LINKS and CON-TACTS. As a newcomer to SAP PA, you can stay with the default DI-RECTED. The links will be displayed going from source to target nodes, which is typically the way you want it, at least at this early stage.

Conditions for link creation

1. **Minimum contacts count**: This number represents the minimum number of relationships between source and target to create a link in your graph. This variable is relevant only for the CONTACTS type of graph.

2. **Use a weight column**: You can select a field from the drop-down to use as a weighted column.

3. **Minimum weight**: You will set the minimum weight needed to create a link.

4. **Maximum number of connections**: You specify the maximum number of connections that SAP PA should create for a node. Once this threshold is reached in the graph, no new connections will be created.

3.4.3 Recommendation

This functionality is closely related to the social analysis we discussed in Section 3.4.2. It enables you to generate product recommendations based on the outputs generated in the social analysis. When you go back to the landing page of SAP PA and click on the RECOMMENDATION link it takes you to the screen shown in Figure 3.52.

Figure 3.52: Landing page for generating recommendations

To create a new recommender, click CREATE A NEW RECOMMENDER You will see a screen similar to what is shown in Figure 3.53.

Figure 3.53: Providing data to a new recommender

75

Provide the same retail data set as the events file. Click ANALYZE to browse the metadata and make any updates as needed. This is shown in Figure 3.54.

	Name	Storage	Value	Key	Order	Missing	Group	Description
1	Category	string	nominal	0	0			
2	Lines	string	nominal	0	0			
3	Ctr	string	nominal	0	0			
4	Country	string	nominal	0	0			
5	Date	datetime	continuous	0	1			
6	Manager	string	nominal	0	0			
7	Quantity sold	number	continuous	0	0			
8	Sales Revenue	number	continuous	0	0			
9	Gross Margin	number	continuous	0	0			
10	Discount	number	continuous	0	0			
11	Customer Satisfaction	number	continuous	0	0			
12	Number of Issues reported	number	continuous	0	0			
13	Comments	string	nominal	0	0			
14	GMR	number	continuous	0	0			
15	Year-Quarter	string	nominal	0	0			
16	KeIndex	integer	continuous	1	0			Automatically a

Figure 3.54: Analyzing the metadata

Now click NEXT to move to the screen shown in Figure 3.55.

Figure 3.55: Configuring the recommender

The important components here are USER and ITEM. In the user field, use a field that corresponds to something like a customer since recommender basically works best for product recommendations. In this case, the field CATEGORY comes closest. The item field should correspond to the kind of product that the customer bought. In this case, the variable LINES works best. The WEIGHT category is optional but helps make the results more useful—if you select an appropriate parameter. Select NUMBER OF ISSUES REPORTED. It is mandatory to provide a date field. In this case, we have a field exactly named DATE. You can also put a time window to your data set by selecting start and end dates. The final parameter is BEST SELLERS. The number you input represents the number above which items are deemed best sellers. The default is 50,000. Change this to 100 because 50,000 is a very high threshold for our data set. Click NEXT. See Figure 3.56.

Figure 3.56: Assigning parameters for recommendation

There are many menu items here. Display the first one, RECOMMENDER because this is the most important one. Let's stay with the defaults and click NEXT to get to the screen shown in Figure 3.57.

77

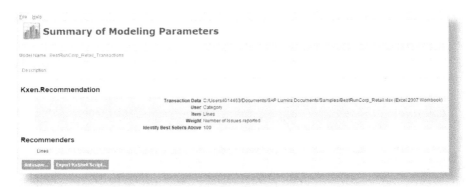

Figure 3.57: Summary of modeling parameters

You see a summary of the modeling parameters, which is more of an FYI screen. Clicking NEXT moves you to the screen showing an overview of the training model. See Figure 3.58.

Model Overview

Overview

Building Date:	2018-09-22 18:32:12	
Learning Time:	2 s	
Engine Name:	Kxen.Recommendation	
Author:	I014463	

Details

Recommenders: Kxen.Recommendation

Lines

Items	0	
Rules	0	
Filtered Line Count	0	

Transactions

Transactions: Kxen.Recommendation

Transactions

Nb of Separate Users	34	
Nb of Separate Items	12	
Nb of UserItem Pairs	35	
Filtered Line Count	16,317	
Nb of Best Sellers	0	

Figure 3.58: Training model overview

You should take note of a few important statistics here. The number of separate users is 34. This means that we have 34 unique categories of products. The number of separate items is listed as 12. This means that we have 12 separate lines of products. Clicking NEXT takes you to the screen shown in Figure 3.59.

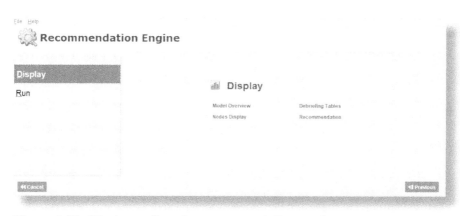

Figure 3.59: Display options in recommendation engine

At this stage, you are training the model and really simulating the results. You have a few options to browse the model and data. However, it makes more sense to actually run your model. So click RUN. See Figure 3.60.

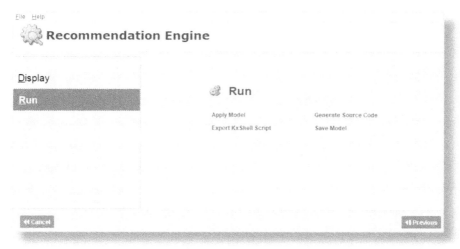

Figure 3.60: Preparing for running the model

Click APPLY MODEL. You will see the screen shown in Figure 3.61.

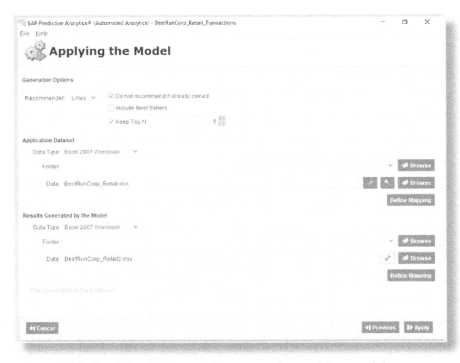

Figure 3.61: Providing folder and file names for applying model

You need to provide the source folder and data file and target folder and data file. Click APPLY. The model will run to completion, successfully, as shown in Figure 3.62.

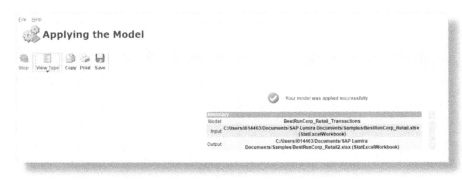

Figure 3.62: Completion notification for model run

When you select VIEW TYPE from the bottom of the screen, as shown in Figure 3.62, the results display in tabular and graphical formats, along with aggregated and detailed information.

3.5 Expert analytics

In the previous sections, you became familiar with the various components of Automated Analytics—the SAP PA component that is suited to the business or casual user. I will now move to the second major category of SAP PA called Expert Analytics. As discussed in Chapter 2, Expert Analytics is the traditional predictive analytics application that has been enhanced over the past few years and is targeted to the data scientist and statistical analyst community. And although you do not truly need a degree in data science to be a productive user of Expert Analytics, a high degree of comfort with the technical aspects of data mining and a statistical programming language such as R, would certainly accelerate your usage of this application.

So what are the key features of Expert Analytics that would serve to attract the more statistically minded users?

Types of operation

You have the following types of operations: classification, clustering, decision trees, neural networks, outliers, regression, and time series.

Classification

Classification is a very popular data mining technique. SAP PA comes with built-in algorithms that help classify the data set into specific groups. A common type of classification is auto classification—this method identifies the best possible binary classification model that predicts the category for data that is not part of the data set. This is done automatically by an algorithm and key input variables to select the best model. You will notice three other classification types. These are to improve the accuracy of your predictive model.

CORE COMPONENTS AND UNITS

Clustering

A popular technique that utilizes algorithms to identify areas of heavy population automatically or clusters based on a target variable.

Decision Tree

A decision tree is a very common classification and regression technique in predictive analytics and therefore, also commonly used in machine learning. A simple and hierarchical (think branches of a tree) set of questions is posed to the data set in order to categorize the data into various buckets. Both the input and output variables can be discrete or continuous in nature. A simple example of the usage of such a decision tree is a series of questions that could lead to whether a company should invest in drilling for oil at a certain location. There are two kinds of decision trees—classification trees and regression trees. When the outcome is nominal such as a *yes* or *no* answer, such a decision tree is a classification tree. The oil drilling example would be a classification tree. Decision trees that have a numeric outcome are regression trees. If, for example, I wanted to predict the net present value (NPV) of a certain amount of investment into an oil well, that would be a regression tree.

Neural networks

A neural network, as the name might suggest, mimics the network of neurons in the human brain and its workings. The intent is for neural networks to be able to learn (i.e. utilize machine learning) so that they become intelligent enough to mimic a human brain. It is a commonly used technique in both predictive analytics and machine learning. Each neural network consists of an input layer (representing the inputs), a hidden layer, and an output layer. The hidden layer is a set of algorithms.

Outliers

These are values in data sets that present anomalies because they deviate significantly from the general behavior of the data set. Presence of outliers tend to skew your observations and analysis because of the undue influence they may exert on your entire data population.

Here is a simple example: You are trying to do product placement for a certain area based on certain characteristics of the data set. One characteristic is *net worth*. You find that in a predominantly lower-middle-class area, there is one resident with a net worth of billions. This person's presence can significantly skew your results, so in your outlier analysis, you may want to exclude this individual from consideration.

Regression

Regression is an umbrella term in statistical analysis, data mining, and predictive analysis that refers to algorithms, techniques, and processes that explore relationships among variables. It is often also the case that regression analysis establishes that there is no relationship between two or more variables. The terminology that is used are *dependent variables* and *independent variables*. Independent variables are the input variables and dependent variables are the output variables. The following types of regression analysis are available to you in SAP PA:

▶ Auto regression

▶ Exponential regression

▶ Geometric regression

▶ Linear regression

▶ Logarithmic regression

Time series

A time series, as the name might suggest, plots variables in a data set as a function of time. Analysis of a time series helps in exploring relationships among variables. It is very commonly used in weather predictions where observations from the past are used to not only explore relationships but also extrapolate future events. There are two kinds of time series: *frequency domain* and *time domain*.

Within each of these operations, you have multiple options. As an example, you can do the following types of classifications in Expert Analytics:

▶ Auto classification

▶ R-bagging classification

▶ R-boosting classification

▶ R-random forecast classification

SAP PA comes prepackaged with a set of predictive algorithms and should those not suffice, you can use the R statistical programming language to create your own

Using sophisticated visual aids, such as decision trees and cluster charts, helps the user interpret the outputs from the training models

Expert Analytics has the following workflow:

Acquire data ⇨ Enrich data ⇨ Predict insights ⇨ Build visualizations ⇨ Explore data ⇨ and Share with your teammates.

When you click the EXPERT ANALYTICS option on the main menu, you see the screen shown in Figure 3.63.

Figure 3.63: Expert Analytics landing page

I will now take you through the sequence steps in Expert Analytics.

3.5.1 Acquiring data

As with any other analytics application, the first step in your predictive journey is data acquisition. This is a straightforward step. Click ACQUIRE DATA to see a list of applications/sources you can acquire your data from, as shown in Figure 3.64.

84

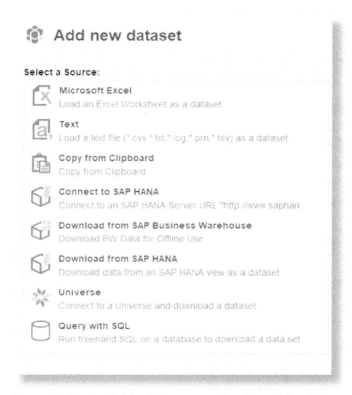

Figure 3.64: Available data sources for Expert Analytics

You currently have a wide range of source systems/applications options for extracting your data. Although this may not seem like a very big list, keep in mind that you can use freehand SQL to download a data set from any SQL-compliant database.

Data acquisition from an SAP HANA database

 There are two SAP HANA-related data acquisition options. It is important to understand both of these. When you connect to SAP HANA, you are not only accessing data in that SAP HANA database but are also able to process your data on that SAP HANA machine/appliance without any data downloaded to your machine. This significantly enhances your processing speed. In the second option, you actually download the

85

data like you would from any other source into your local machine and the processing takes place in your local machine. In this instance, the SAP HANA machine/appliance is merely a source of your data.

Now upload the MS Excel spreadsheet from your hard drive by clicking on the MICROSOFT EXCEL link shown in Figure 3.64 and then clicking NEXT to get to the interface where you will provide the name and location of the spreadsheet. A partial screenshot of the acquired data is shown in Figure 3.65.

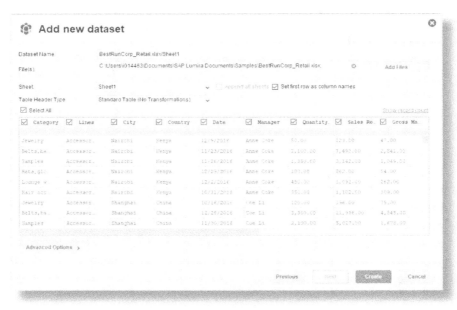

Figure 3.65: Adding a new data set in Expert Analytics

This interface offers you some opportunities for managing your data set. If you uncheck the SELECT ALL flag, you can specify the fields/columns you want to extract. By clicking ADVANCED OPTIONS, you can control how hidden rows and columns (if any) are handled. To merge data sets, click ADD FILES.

Once satisfied with the data, click CREATE. Expert Analytics will now physically create this data set in its database. The next phase is to enrich the data.

3.5.2 Enriching the data

In this phase, the imported data can be massaged and enhanced to make it more useful for your analysis. Some of the activities you might want to do in this phase are creating a new measure based on an existing dimension or column, performing data conversions (such as converting data in date format to non-date if date is not critical to your analysis), and adding geographical coordinates to your data (meaning latitude and longitude) using the state, city, and zip codes as the base information.

Scrubbing your data set

 If your data has not previously been cleansed and/or deduplicated, here is where such data discrepancies are detected and where you can rectify them.

Some of the enrichment activities can be less eventful, such as merging another data set. We already encountered this activity in the previous section. You can do it here, too. Look at the output from the extraction of the data set in the previous screen. Please take your time to soak in this user interface. It is very intuitive but like everything else, the first time you see it there is a lot of information to absorb. You are taken straight to the default VISUALIZE view. It's too early to visualize because we first need to prepare the data. So switch to the PREPARE view by clicking this menu item. You will see the screen shown in Figure 3.66.

Figure 3.66: Prepare view in Expert Analytics

In this view, you can carry out various enrichment activities by clicking one or more of the buttons on the right. To add a new dimension or a new measure, click the appropriate button, as shown in Figure 3.67.

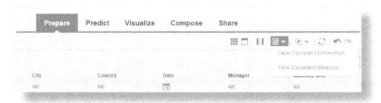

Figure 3.67: Preparing to update/enrich your data set

You have access to a variety of standard functions to create a new dimension or measure including financial, logical, mathematical, and string. If you click the button to the right (with two intersecting circles), you will append or merge two data sets.

You can do a lot more with data enrichment, such as enrichment activities with the CATEGORY dimension for substituting and trimming. It's very easy. Highlight CATEGORY. The application then displays all the data enrichment options on the bottom right-hand side of the screen. This is shown in Figure 3.68.

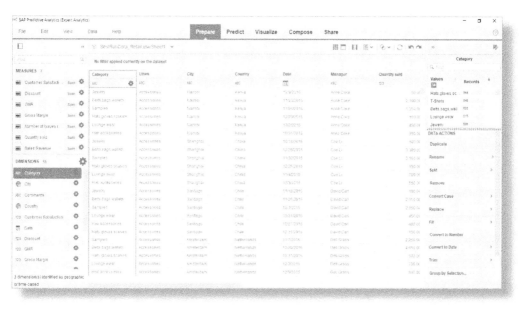

Figure 3.68: Enrichment options for a dimension

To substitute one or more values for this dimension, you need to click RE-PLACE and then enter your desired substitution rule. If you want to do some trimming to the values, click TRIM and then identify the delimiter you would like to trim values on, i.e. colon, semi-colon, comma, and space. One final word on data enrichment. SAP Analytics Cloud (SAC) has intelligence built into it that allows it to detect any geographical field. If you look back at Figure 3.68, you will see three dimensions that have been identified as geographic or time-based. Using these, the system will provide geographical coordinates (latitudes and longitudes) for each of the data points. The accuracy of these coordinates is directly proportional to the specificity of the geographical data. If you only have two high-level geographical dimensions (like city and country, in this case), the coordinates will correspond to the coordinates of the center of the city. Assuming geospatial analysis is not the primary objective of your analysis, this level of geographical detail will suffice.

Once you are satisfied with your data set, you can move onto the predictive aspects. Select the PREDICT menu item and you will be taken to a screen similar to the one shown in Figure 3.69.

89

Figure 3.69: Predictive algorithms

Take notice of the area outlined with a red box. This is where you will find the all the predictive and data mining functions that SAP delivers out of the box. To do predictive analytics on your data set, you will need to apply one or more predictive functions from this box. If you are a regular business user, you will have more than what you need for your predictive analytics needs. SAP delivers a pretty impressive suite of algorithms that includes the ability to do association, classification, clustering, decision trees, neural networks, outliers, regression, and time-series analysis.

Before you proceed, you may want to do some statistical preparation or preprocessing of your data set. This is not to be confused with the data enrichment done in the previous step. Without this step, your data set may not be ready for a predictive algorithm to be applied. Figure 3.70 shows the standard preprocessing functions SAP provides.

Expand the ALGORITHMS node. Look at the prepackaged functionality. A partial screenshot is shown in Figure 3.71.

Figure 3.70: Standard preprocessing algorithms

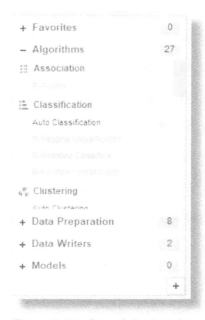

Figure 3.71: Out-of-the-box functionality

Data preparation

Now let's shift our attention to data preparation. This is an important step in the journey to creating predictive models. Using data preparation steps, you can massage and fine-tune your data so that it's in a shape that you can use for applying predictive techniques. In the world of SAP PA, this activity is called *preprocessing of your data set.* Figure 3.72 displays the expanded data preparation node.

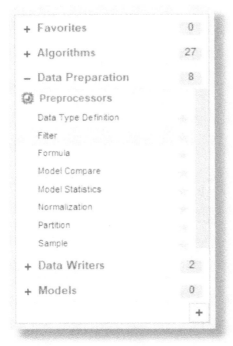

Figure 3.72: Data preparation node

Data type definition

You can use this function to change the field names and types of your data.

Filter

In this activity, you can limit your data to a certain subset based on the filter criteria you apply.

Formula

You can use this capability to create a new calculation on your data. This can either be an existing function or an existing operator that comes built in with SAP PA.

Model compare

In this activity, you compare existing models and select the model that best suits your needs.

Model statistics

This function provides you with the statistics of your data set based on the target column and prediction column you select. You can select either the CLASSIFICATION or REGRESSION ALGORITHM TYPE for statistics. Figure 3.73 shows the screen.

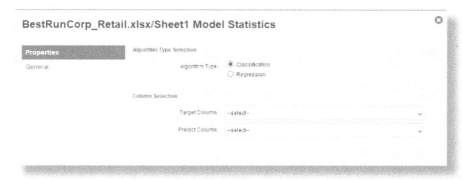

Figure 3.73: Selecting an algorithm

Normalization

Sometimes you only need display one or more of your numerical data (values of one or more fields/columns) in terms of minimum and maximum or some decimal scaling. This is the purpose of normalization. Figure 3.74 shows this.

Figure 3.74: Normalization options

Partition

Using this function, you are able to split your data into three sets—test, train, and validate. You can set parameters to control how large each of these sets should be. Figure 3.75 shows this.

Figure 3.75: Partitioning your data set

There is only one (default) partition method and this is random. In random seeding, you can enter a value not exceeding nine digits. For the data set sizes, you can only enter a value between 1 and 100, and including both of these numbers.

Sample

In this activity, you select a smaller representative data set from your over-all data set. You can set certain parameters to create your sample. There are a few sampling options you can choose from such as FIRST N, LAST N, SIMPLE RANDOM, etc. You can set the number of rows in your sample data set either by specifying the number of rows, or percentage of rows. Optionally, you can also set the maximum number of rows. This is shown in Figure 3.76.

Figure 3.76: Setting the number of rows

If your data set is too large, you may want to use a subset of it. In that case, you can use the SAMPLE function to select the subset. Or you might want to filter on certain dimensions or values of the data set. In that case, you would use the FILTER function. It allows you to do a row, a column, or a general filter. You can apply formulas, or normalize or partition your data set. More on this in Chapter 4.

One final thing that I'd like to mention here is that you are not limited to using the prepackaged algorithms and function delivered by SAP. You can start adding your own models by clicking the "+" button.

Of course you will want to view the output of the predictive models in a more visual way. So it is now time to move on from the PREDICT view to the VISUALIZE view. This is shown in Figure 3.77.

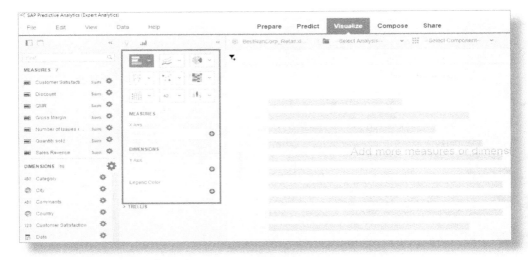

Figure 3.77: Visualize view

You will notice a blank canvas on the right and the metadata on the left. In between, in the area outlined by the red box, there are the various chart options. Depending on the chart type you select, you will be prompted to add a minimum number of dimensions and measures to make your analysis meaningful.

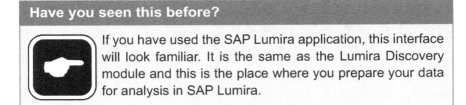

Have you seen this before?

If you have used the SAP Lumira application, this interface will look familiar. It is the same as the Lumira Discovery module and this is the place where you prepare your data for analysis in SAP Lumira.

Chart types

Now look at each of the chart types to get a sense of the immense visualization possibilities you have.

Bar and column charts

You currently are able to pick from seven bar and columns chart types. See Figure 3.78.

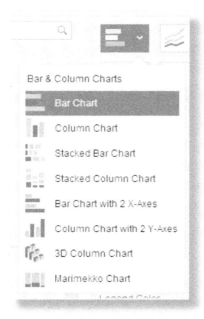

Figure 3.78: Various bar and column chart options

Line charts

There are five types of line charts that you can currently pick from. See Figure 3.79.

Figure 3.79: Line chart options

Pie charts

With pie charts, you have three options—regular PIE CHART, DONUT CHART, and PIE WITH DEPTH CHART. See Figure 3.80.

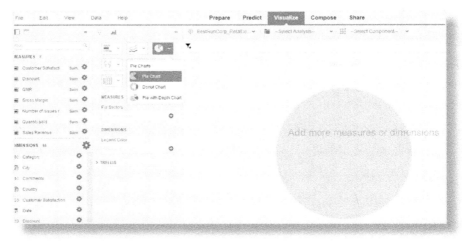

Figure 3.80: Pie chart options

Geographic charts

Expert Analytics comes prepackaged with four types of geographic charts as shown in Figure 3.81.

Figure 3.81: Geographic chart options

Scatter charts

Expert Analytics comes prepackaged with three types of charts/graphs as shown in Figure 3.82.

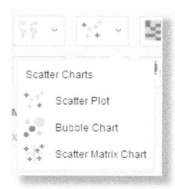

Figure 3.82: Scatter chart options

Map charts

There are two kinds of map charts available in Expert Analytics. See Figure 3.83.

Figure 3.83: Map chart options

99

Tables

There are two kinds of table options as shown in Figure 3.84.

Figure 3.84: Table options

Point chart

There is one type of point chart available, as shown in Figure 3.85.

Figure 3.85: Point chart options

Other charts

There is a smorgasbord of various charts that do not fall into other categories. Some of these chart types have been added in recent releases. Your
current options are shown in Figure 3.86.

Figure 3.86: All the other chart types

After going through this long list of visualization options, I am sure you would agree that there is no shortage of options. And if that weren't enough, SAP typically adds new chart types in new releases, thus further expanding your options.

When to use which chart type?

 I am often asked what chart type one should use for analysis. This is a difficult question to answer because choosing the right type is as much a science as it as an art. And what is right can be described as some poet described beauty: it lies in the eyes of the beholder. Nonetheless, my recommendation is not to get carried away with the bells and whistles, but focus your KPIs. If you are new to this area, start simple and go for basic types like line graphs and pie charts.

Here are a couple of other observations. Adding measures and dimensions to your visualization is simple. You can click the "+" button next to the corresponding box, or drag and drop the type to the appropriate location. Based on the chart type you select, your options will change. Let's say you choose a bubble chart. Figure 3.87 shows the options you will be presented with for setting up your visualization.

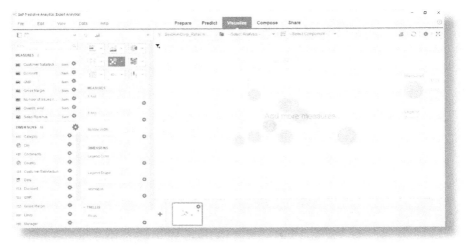

Figure 3.87: Preparing to visualize

This set of visualization options has some differences with those for, say, a bar graph.

There is a constant presence in all of these screens. It is *Trellis*. A trellis is like a mash-up and enables you to place a set of charts side-by-side for comparison.

Compose

Let's move on to the next phase, COMPOSE. This is where you do your storytelling. In this function, you bring together all your visualizations and weave them together into a coherent narrative. Figure 3.88 displays the screen you will see when you click COMPOSE.

Figure 3.88: Getting ready to compose a story

There are three options for composing your story—INFOGRAPHIC, BOARD, and REPORT.

1. Infographic

Infographic is the initial/default option. The concept of infographic is fairly commonplace. It combines graphics and text to convey a powerful message. You can choose from the following types of template canvases: BLANK, STANDARD, OVERVIEW, and DETAILED. Which one you choose depends on the type of message you are trying to convey. As an example, to create an infographic with explanations accompanying your graphics, you may want to use the DETAILED template. Let's see how this looks. Figure 3.89 shows a template.

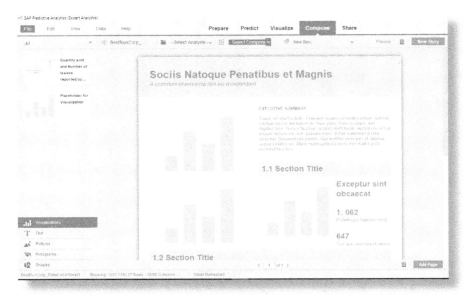

Figure 3.89: Available template for storytelling

Although it may be difficult to figure out, you can replace all the content with your own content by dragging the object/component of your choice and dropping it on your canvas. On the bottom left corner of the screen are the various components you can drag.

2. Board

You typically use the board type of storytelling for presenting aggregated information. It is a collection of visualizations with user-defined filters. A key distinguishing characteristic is the usage of interactive charts. Figure 3.90 displays the various options you have when you select this mode.

You can select from six templates, including a blank one. Now let's look at one of the templates that is generated. Figure 3.91 displays the RIGHT template.

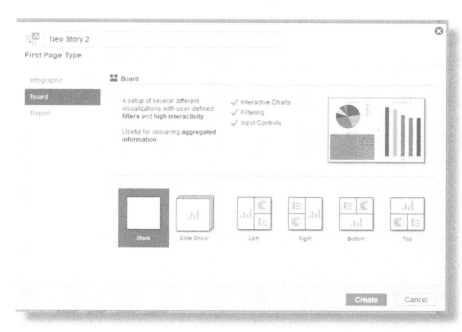

Figure 3.90: Storytelling types with the board option

Figure 3.91: Right template screen

There are many capabilities here. You can drag and drop various charts, text, images, and input controls. Input controls enable interactivity. You can set up one or more filters based on values of existing dimensions. You'll notice two filters in Figure 3.92, one for DISCOUNT and one for GROSS MARGIN. You can control the data that is displayed based by the filters you you select.

Figure 3.92: Adding controls to a right template

You can impart various color schemes by choosing colors from the pallete located on the far right corner of the page.

Combining storyboarding types

You can mix and match various types of storyboarding. The NEW PAGE button lets you do exactly that. You can stick to the same template and add additional pages of information that you can then present to your audience in the form of a package or a presentation.

---

3. Report

The report type of storyboard is basically a blank canvas where you bring everything together. As such, it has only one template and it is the blank one. See Figure 3.93.

Figure 3.93: Report option

Let's move to the final activity—dissemination of your package/story. SAP provides many options to share your package. Let's look at these options by clicking SHARE. See Figure 3.94.

Figure 3.94: Preparing to distribute your story

The EXPORT AS FILE option is the most obvious option and helps you save your package as a static file that can be shared via email or uploaded to a shared folder or drive. The other options require you to provide system and user credentials. For example, to publish to an SAP HANA server, you will need to provide credentials, as shown in Figure 3.95.

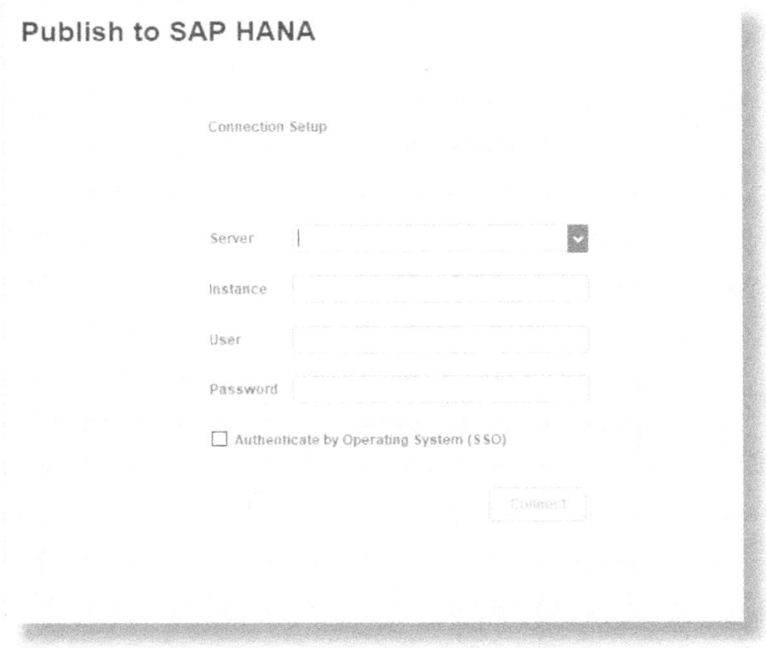

Publish to SAP HANA

Connection Setup

Server

Instance

User

Password

☐ Authenticate by Operating System (SSO)

Connect

Figure 3.95: Getting ready to publish your story to an SAP HANA platform

The good news is that you don't have to provide these credentials each time you publish. Check the box AUTHENTICATE BY OPERATING SYSTEM (SSO) to have information retained.

Where to publish?

 Not too long ago, publishing such presentations on a corporate intranet portal was fairly common. It isn't any longer. Such material is now published to publicly accessible media such as the cloud, SAP HANA platform, SAP StreamWork, and so on.

108

3.6 Toolkit

The toolkit consists of a set of utility functions that you will want to execute more than once. Figure 3.96 displays the list of these utilities.

Figure 3.96: Options available in toolkit

Let's look at each one of these functions is some detail.

3.6.1 Open the data viewer

This function is self-explanatory. You can browse your data set. Click OPEN THE DATA VIEWER. See Figure 3.97.

Figure 3.97: Opening the data viewer

You will need to specify the folder and the file. SAP PA keeps track of the data sets you've recently accessed. Highlight the file of data you want to browse and then click the VIEW DATA button. Figure 3.98 displays a partial screenshot that is generated by SAP PA.

Figure 3.98: Viewing data

If you prefer a statistical view of your data, you can click the STATISTICS button. If you would like to get a graphical view of your data, you can click the GRAPH button. Let's do that. Figure 3.99 shows the resulting screen.

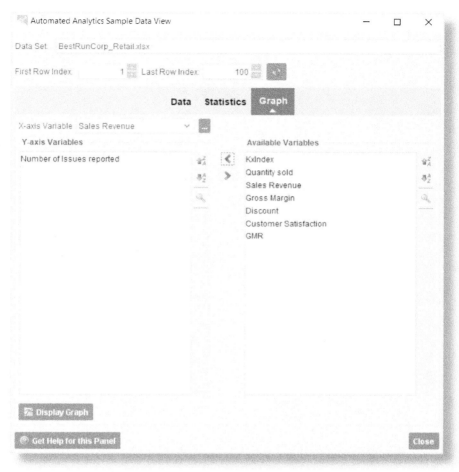

Figure 3.99: Getting ready to display data in graphical view

To visualize the quality of the product sold as a function of the sales revenue, specify these fields as the Y and X axes respectively, then click DIS-
PLAY GRAPH. Figure 3.100 displays the graph that is generated.

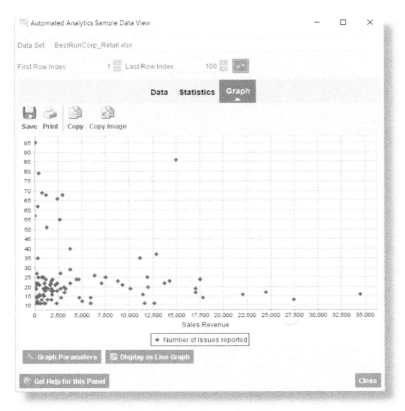

Figure 3.100: Graphical view of sample data

Note that this graph is based on the first 100 records, not the entire data set.

Visualization overdose?

 SAP PA has good visualization capabilities. It is common to overlook these features for all the predictive algorithms that run in the background. It is a good idea to use these visualization capabilities to get a better overall idea of your data.

3.6.2 Perform a data transfer

Using this function, you can transfer some or all of your data set into another format or simply replicate it. Click on PERFORM A DATA TRANSFER. See Figure 3.101.

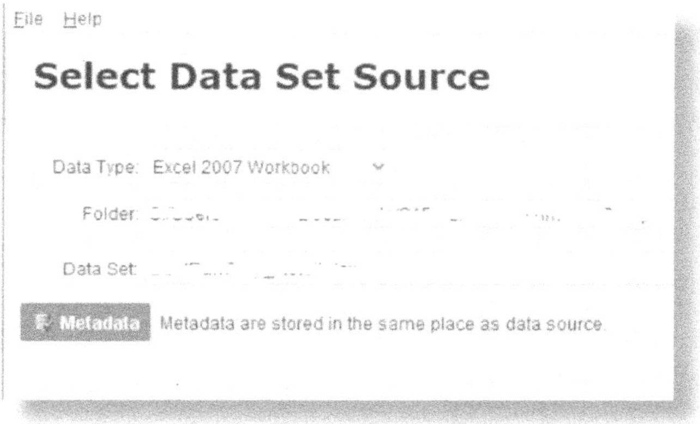

Figure 3.101: Identifying data source for data load

Provide the folder and name of the file for the retail data set. Click the NEXT button and you will go to the familiar DESCRIBE DATA SET screen, as shown in Figure 3.102.

Figure 3.102: Getting ready to analyze metadata

Analyze that!

This screen in Figure 3.102 is a primary interface to many other SAP PA activities. SAP prompts you to analyze the data in case you have forgotten to do it. Unless you analyze the data, you will not be able to go to the next activity.

After analyzing the data, click NEXT to move to the screen to identify the fields to include in the target data set. This is shown in Figure 3.103.

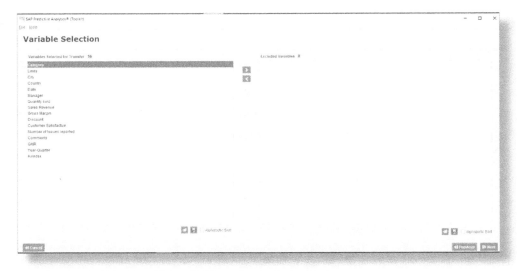

Figure 3.103: Identifying fields to be included in target

Here, you can exclude one or more fields and save both the included and excluded lists for future reference. When you are ready to proceed, click NEXT. See Figure 3.104.

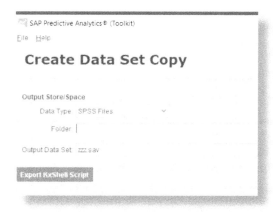

Figure 3.104: Create data set copy

Now you need to identify the type of format you want your source data set to be saved in. To store it as an SPSS file, select that option from the DATA TYPE drop-down and then select the folder where your target file is to be saved. SAP PA automatically appends the .sav file name extension to the output data file. Give your file a name and do not change the file name extension. Now click NEXT. See Figure 3.105.

Figure 3.105: Getting ready to view results following successful data transfer

115

Assuming there are no errors, SAP PA will generate a new file and you can view the output.

3.6.3 List distinct values in a data set

Now go back to the landing page for Tookit (shown in Figure 3.96). The 3rd option is LIST DISTINCT VALUES IN A DATA SET. You would use this function to get a list of unique values in your data set. Once you click this link, it will take you to the usual interface where you need to provide the name of the file. Use the retail data file. You will be taken to the next screen (seen a few times before) where you do the mandatory data analysis. Once you do that, you will be prompted to select the fields you want extracted. To see the unique cities in this data set, check the box next to CITY, as shown in Figure 3.106.

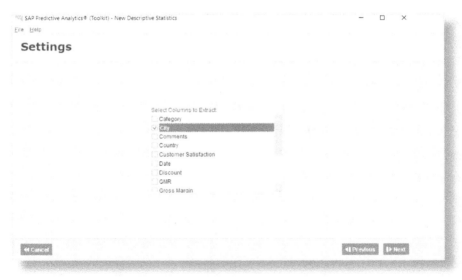

Figure 3.106: Making appropriate sets

Click the NEXT button to go to the screen to specify the format and location of the output file. This is shown in Figure 3.107.

Save the output as an MS Excel workbook. Click NEXT. SAP PA will process the data set and return the list of unique values for this data set. A partial screenshot of this is shown in Figure 3.108.

Figure 3.107: Specifying location and name of output file

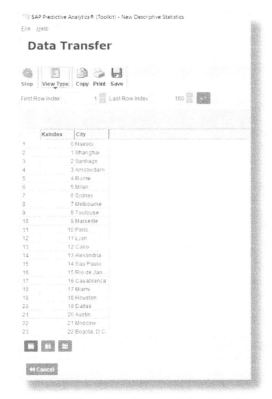

Figure 3.108: List of unique cities in data set

3.6.4　Get descriptive statistics for a data set

This useful function allows you to extract a variety of statistical information on your data set. It helps you understand the relationship between various components in your data. You will designate one or more fields from your data set as source (or explanatory) variables and one or more fields/variables as the target variable(s). SAP PA will run algorithms to figure out the relationship among these variables. What is the purpose of doing this? Before applying predictive models on your data, it is a good idea for you to get a basic understanding of these relationships. As an example, if (source) variable A has little to no impact on (target) variable B, it is not useful to build a predictive model around this relationship. Conversely, by running this function, you may detect relationships among fields that you were not aware of and would probably not have included in your predictive model.

So, let's look at how this works. Click GET DESCRIPTIVE STATISTICS FOR A DATA SET. It will take you to the screen where you specify the location and name of the file containing the retail data set. In the next screen, do the mandatory analysis of the data set, and then go the next screen. Here is where you will set up your cause and effect relationships. Retain the fields/variables on the left panel whose contribution to the target you want to analyze, EXPLANATORY VARIABLES SELECTED, and move the EFFECT field(s)/column(s) to the TARGET VARIABLE panel. You can select one field as the WEIGHT VARIABLE. Do so judiciously—a weight variable should be a numeric field and it helps to disaggregate the combined value of the explanatory variable. You should move all fields/columns that you do not want as part of the cause-effect relationship to the excluded variable list.

To understand the impact that sales revenue has on the number of issues reported, specify QUANTITY SOLD as the WEIGHT VARIABLE. Exclude all the other fields from consideration. See Figure 3.109.

Now that you have done your preparation, let the application take over and do the hard work for you. Click NEXT. See Figure 3.110.

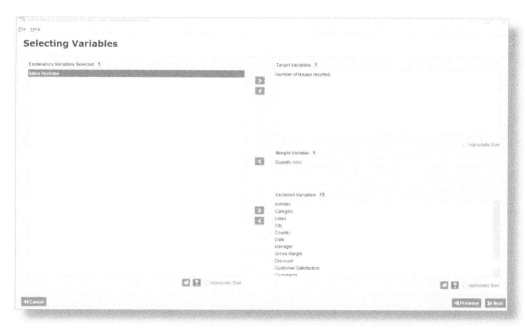

Figure 3.109: Identifying the explanatory and target variables

On this screen, give your model an appropriate title and a meaningful description. You can do an AUTOSAVE—this is a good practice because your model will be stored each time you generate it. The export option allows you to save the generated Kx shell script for future re-use.

If you are satisfied with your preparation, you can click NEXT to go to the STATISTICS DEBRIEFING screen, as shown in Figure 3.111, where you can select how to view the output of the statistical analysis.

Figure 3.111: Choosing mode of a statistical display

Only relevant options will be available for selection. The SUMMARY option is obvious—you will see key information of your parameters. One option of high interest could be CATEGORY SIGNIFICANCE. It will tell you how close a relationship is between the explanatory variable(s) and the target. The STATISTICAL REPORTS option will allow you to display the outputs in a variety of different statistical formats.

Click CATEGORY SIGNIFICANCE to understand the relationship between sales revenue and number of issues reported. Figure 3.112 shows the graph.

SAP PA displays the bar chart view by default. The contribution is relative to the mean of the target category. The positive bars denote more than the mean number of the target category and is an indicator of a proportional relationship between contributor and target and the negative numbers denote less than the mean number and thus denote an inverse relationship between contributor and target. A value of zero would mean that there is no relationship between the two. In this particular case, from a purely visual assessment, there is no discernible relationship between the two. The positives and the negatives seem to balance out but there is no clear pattern. You can save the tabular information in an MS Excel spreadsheet.

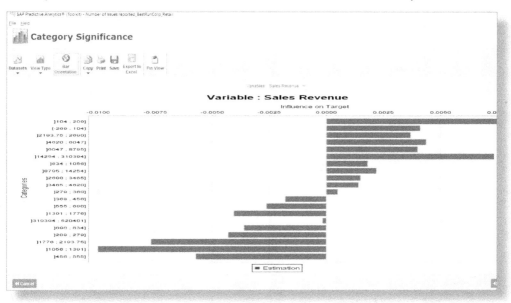

Figure 3.112: Exploring a relationship between variables

If you are done saving and/or copying this information and are ready to move on, click CANCEL to be taken to the TOOLKIT screen.

3.6.5   Compute optimized groups for a target

This final option in the TOOLKIT category is only relevant if your data set has geographical data. It helps you group the input/explanatory variables in relationship with the target variable.

121

4 Predictive analytics: Use cases

In the preceding chapters, I covered the history and evolution of SAP PA, the roadmap, the technical underpinnings, and the functions and features of each of its components. I hope that you now have a fundamental understanding of the conceptual aspects of SAP PA.

SAP PA as a paradigm is pervasive and someday the *P* in *PA* could stand for *pervasive*. It is hard to find any organization today, regardless of size, geography, or industry not to be planning initiatives in the SAP PA space if they are not actively engaged in them. In recent years, every customer I have worked with has shown interest in SAP PA even though the broad topic of discussion and engagement is well removed from SAP PA. Business and/or digital transformation initiatives have SAP PA embedded in them explicitly or implicitly. This is because SAP PA is a vehicle for transformation that allows you to unleash the hidden patterns in your data to bring about positive change in your organization.

Below is a list of the most popular use cases of SAP PA in selected industries. Please note that this list is by no means exhaustive. It is merely intended to give you a sense of the uses the application is being put into.

Banking and industry

- ▶ Reducing customer churn
- ▶ Maximizing cross-selling and upselling opportunities
- ▶ Mitigating risk
- ▶ Fraud detection
- ▶ Increasing ROI of marketing campaigns

Manufacturing

- ▶ Predictive maintenance and quality
- ▶ Product clustering
- ▶ Warranty valuation analysis
- ▶ Analytics for configurable components

Utilities

- ▶ Reduce customer churn
- ▶ Maximize cross-selling and upselling opportunities
- ▶ Forecast demand and supply

Public services

- ▶ Optimize tax collection
- ▶ Improve crime policing
- ▶ Prevent tax fraud
- ▶ Manage urban transportation

Retail and consumer packaged goods

- ▶ Reduce customer churn
- ▶ Recommend products
- ▶ Enable customer segmentation and targeting
- ▶ Increase marketing campaign ROIs

Now look at the most popular SAP PA use cases from a business function/ area standpoint.

Finance

- ▶ Optimization of receivables and payables
- ▶ Financial close optimization
- ▶ Forecasting automation
- ▶ Financial loss prevention
- ▶ Advanced KPI forecasting

Sales and marketing

- ▶ Sales/pipeline forecasting
- ▶ Customer churn reduction
- ▶ Customer acquisition optimization

- ▶ Price optimization
- ▶ Product affinity analysis

Human resources

- ▶ Reduce employee churn
- ▶ Identify and retain top talent
- ▶ Improve managerial performance
- ▶ Project training costs

Operations

- ▶ Predictive maintenance/asset management
- ▶ Demand forecast
- ▶ Workforce analytics
- ▶ Cannibalization effects of promotions

4.1 Use case: Sales/pipeline forecasting

It is now time to segue into a practical discussion and illustration of SAP PA. Since the data set you have been using throughout this book is from a (fictitious) retail company and therefore consists of retail data, good topics for predictive analytics are customer segmentation and sales/pipeline forecasting. The data set we have been using does not have customer data, but it has a sizeable amount of sales data from a product standpoint. A sales manager or supervisor would be interested in understanding the hidden patterns in this data and making intelligent forecasts and predictions on what needs to be done to increase sales.

> **It's easy**
>
> The purpose of a *proof of concept* is to emphasize, illustrate, and underscore the fact that you do not need to be a data scientist to utilize predictive analytics. All you need to do is to feed the right parameters and criteria to the application and let the predictive algorithms take over.

Expert Analytics in SAP PA unburdens you of any heavy lifting. Your responsibility is to know what you want, and specify the correct inputs, outputs, and type of analytics you want to do.

Let's run SAP PA. Click the EXPERT ANALYTICS menu option, as shown in Figure 4.1.

Figure 4.1: SAP PA for Expert Analytics

Now click the EXPERT ANALYTICS menu item that is in tiny print and hyperlinked. See Figure 4.2.

Figure 4.2: Expert Analytics landing page

The first step is to acquire data for analysis. Click ACQUIRE DATA to move to the next screen, as shown in Figure 4.3.

All your recently used files will show up on the right panel. If you don't want to pick from a recent file or do not have a recent file, select a source from

126

the left panel. The retail data set is in MS Excel format so click MICROSOFT EXCEL and point to the local folder in which the file is situated. A subset of the data will be available, as shown in Figure 4.4.

Figure 4.3: Data acquisition options

Figure 4.4: Preview of acquired data set

127

Click CREATE and navigate to the PREPARE tab. This is shown in Figure 4.5.

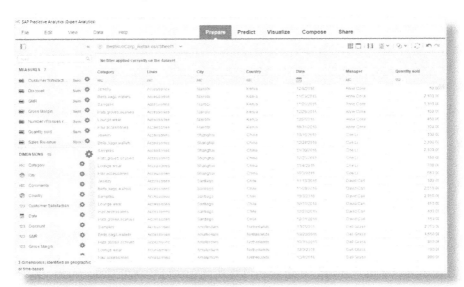

Figure 4.5: Preparing your data

The data preparation step is an important one. Here you have the opportunity to clean up, enhance, and fine-tune your data set in case you are
not satisfied with the raw data. It is almost certain that there will always be
things you will want to tweak in your raw data set. A few improvements and
enhancements to make to this data set are:

▶ Rename the GROSS MARGIN field PROFIT

▶ Rename GMR to RETURN ON SALES (%)

▶ Eliminate the unnecessary precision in the QUANTITY SOLD and
NUMBER OF ISSUES fields (there is no need for decimal points here)

▶ Rename CUSTOMER SATISFACTION to CUSTOMER SATISFACTION %

Figure 4.6 displays a partial screenshot of the enriched data set.

Figure 4.6: Enriched data set

Now click PREDICT to set up your parameters and functions for doing predictive analytics on your retail data set. It will display the screen shown in Figure 4.7.

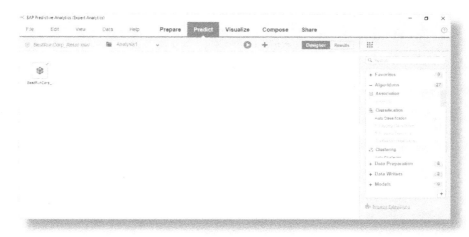

Figure 4.7: Getting ready to do predictive analytics on your data set

You will be presented with a somewhat blank canvas that has your data set as the only object. On this canvas, you will have the opportunity to build your predictive model by dragging the algorithm or function you want to apply to your data set and dropping it on the canvas. When I introduced you to Expert Anaytics earlier, I mentioned that this application does not require you to be a data scientist. I will now illustrate why that is the case.

One of the options you have is DATA PREPARATION. You can use functions in this section to augment your data in terms of additional fields using formulas, filtering, normalization, partitioning, creating subsets, etc. Drag and drop the formula operator to create a new column that shows the % of issues reported per quantity sold. This is shown in Figure 4.8.

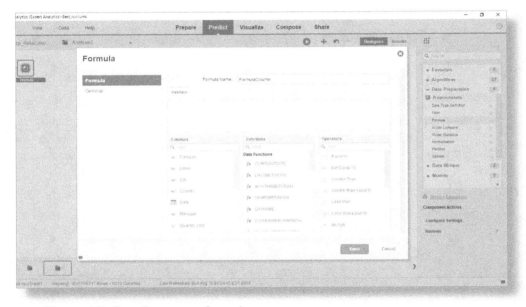

Figure 4.8: Creating a new formula

Double-click the numerator NUMBER OF ISSUES from the COLUMNS panel and then double-click DIVISION from the OPERATORS panel and then double-click the NUMERATOR field QUANTITY SOLD. See Figure 4.9.

Click DONE and then click the green arrow button to execute this job. Switch to the RESULTS tab. A partial screenshot is shown in Figure 4.10.

Figure 4.9: Providing operators and operands to your formula

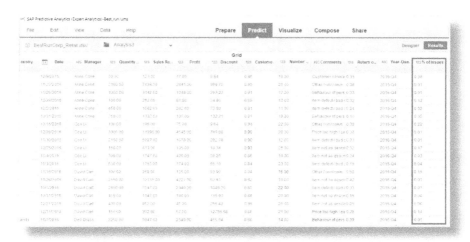

Figure 4.10: Results of applying the formula to a data set

A new column with values based on the formula we just assigned has been created. (This new column is outlined with a red box for easy identification).

4.1.1 Auto clustering

Now we can do some clustering analysis. Switch back to DESIGNER mode and drag and drop AUTO CLUSTERING into the canvas and connect the output of the formula to this step. This is shown in Figure 4.11.

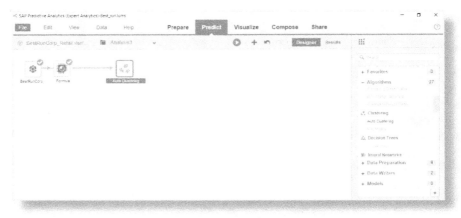

Figure 4.11: Including auto clustering into the analysis workflow

Double-click the AUTO CLUSTERING function on the canvas to understand the correlation between the profit and customer satisfaction and number of issues reported. Check the appropriate checkboxes in the FEATURES panel.

Variable is auto clustering

 There are two types of variables in auto clustering: independent and dependent. The columns available for selection in the FEATURES panel are all independent variables/ fields. The target variable is deemed to be dependent because you want to understand how one or more of the independent variables affects the target/dependent variable.

Also select MANAGER and COUNTRY fields as input variables. This is to illustrate that non-numeric input variables are not taken into account by the auto clustering algorithm.

Select PROFIT as the target variable. In the OUTPUT INFORMATION panel, specify the minimum and maximum number of clusters you want the algorithm to generate. There are really no guidelines to this—what numbers you set depends on the level of granularity you want your data to be displayed in. Finally, assign a new column name for the new data that will be generated. All of this is shown in Figure 4.12.

Figure 4.12: Supplying parameters for auto clustering

Now click DONE and then RESULTS as shown with red outline in Figure 4.13.

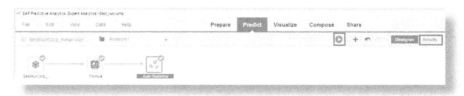

Figure 4.13: Getting ready to run auto clustering

By default, you will be taken to a tabular view of the data. Figure 4.14 displays a partial screenshot of the results.

133

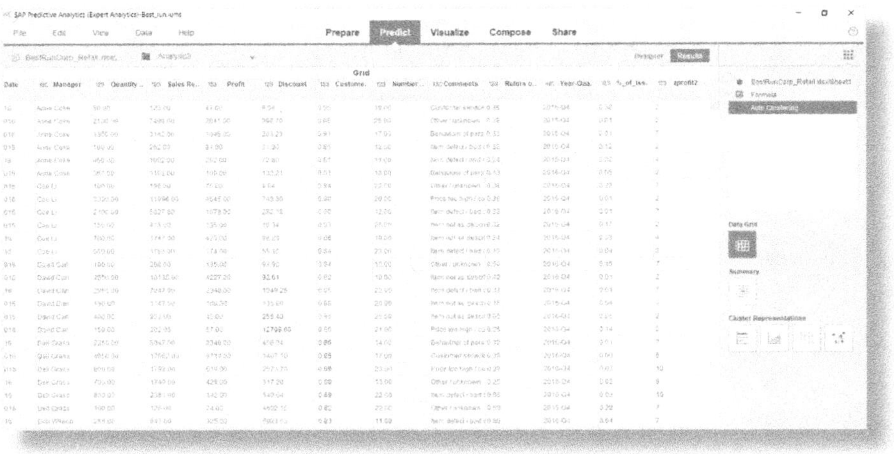

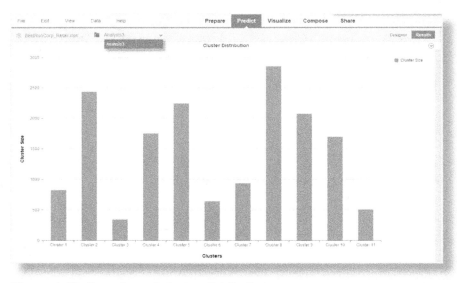

Figure 4.14: Tablular view of results from auto clustering

I would like to draw your attention to the newly generated profit column (zprofit2). At a glance, you can tell that SAP PA has grouped your target variable (profit) into clusters. This representation is not too meaningful. To get a visual overview of the results, you can select one or more of the options under CLUSTER REPRESENTATION. We will select all four. Click the first button CLUSTER DISTRIBUTION ▦. This is shown in Figure 4.15.

Figure 4.15: Overview of cluster distribution

Now click the second button FEATURE DISTRIBUTION. Figure 4.16 displays the output.

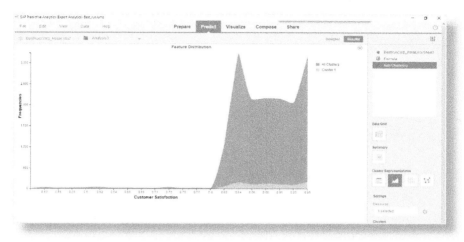

Figure 4.16: Feature distribution of clustered data

SAP PA has selected the variable CUSTOMER SATISFACTION by default. By clicking the "+" under MEASURES, you can switch to the other numeric input variable, NUMBER OF ISSUES REPORTED. The result is shown in Figure 4.17.

Figure 4.17: Switching to another numeric input variable

135

Now switch to the third chart option PARALLEL COORDINATE CHART . When you click this button, you see a screen similar to the one shown in Figure 4.18.

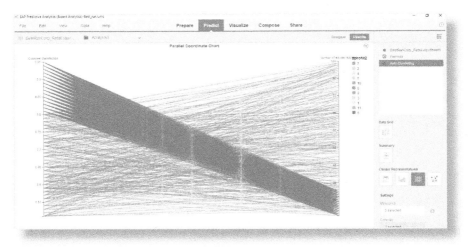

Figure 4.18: Parallel coordinate chart

Notice (at the bottom right corner of the screenshot) that two measures have been preselected.

> ## Prerequisite for using the parallel coordinate chart
>
> To utilize the parallel coordinate chart graph type in Auto Clustering, you must have at least two measures available in your data set and at least two measures selected as input variables.

Now generate the fourth and final graph—the SCATTER MATRIX CHART . Clicking that option will generate a screen similar to what is shown in Figure 4.19.

Figure 4.19: Scatter matrix chart

4.1.2 Auto regression

Let's move onto another popular data mining technique—regression. With auto regression, you can run regression analysis on your data based on the input parameters that you provide the regression algorithm. First, drag the AUTO REGRESSION algorithm from the panel on the right and drop it onto your canvas, as shown in Figure 4.20.

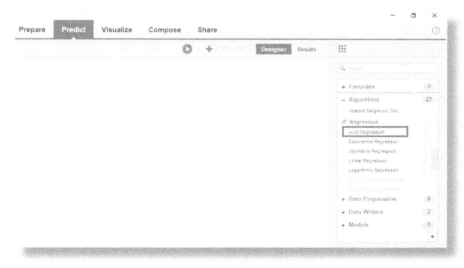

Figure 4.20: Locating the auto regression algorithm

Connect the auto regression algorithm to your data set. This is shown in Figure 4.21.

Figure 4.21: Getting ready to apply auto regression to a data set

Double-click the AUTO REGRESSION function. Review the screen shown in Figure 4.22. Check all the fields whose contribution to the output variable you want to understand. Choosing a target variable is mandatory. Select the NUMBER OF ISSUES REPORTED as the TARGET VARIABLE to see how variables/fields such as quantity sold, sales revenue, profit, etc. contribute to the target variable. Then name the new column that will contain the predicted values.

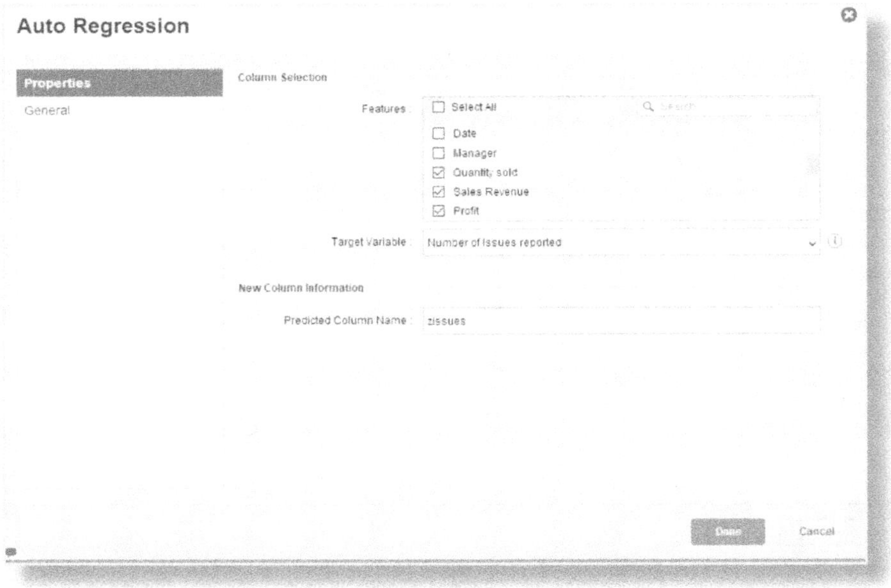

Figure 4.22: Supplying parameters to the algorithm

Click DONE to see the tabular view of the results. This is shown in Figure 4.23.

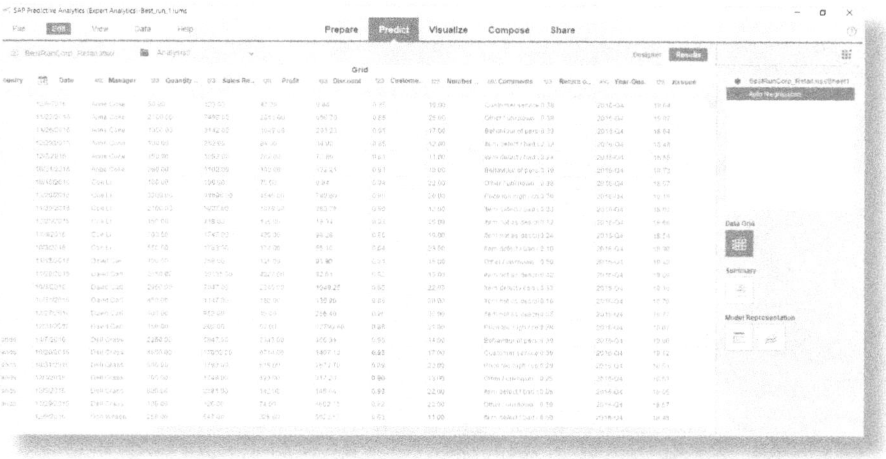

Figure 4.23: Tabluar view of output from application of regression to data set

A tabular display may be of little value. Keep in mind that a large contributor to the value of predictive analytics is visualization. This is especially true when you are mining data for predictive analysis because you are typically handling very large volumes. Therefore, a tabular display of results will lead to little or no analytical value. Thankfully, SAP PA does a lot of the heavy lifting for you. Click the first option under MODEL REPRESENTATION . This is the variables contribution function option. The result is shown in Figure 4.24. You can see how the three contributory variables selected earlier impact the target variable.

The quantity sold has the biggest impact on the number of issues, but somewhat surprisingly, the sales revenue variable has a smaller impact than quantity sold.

Figure 4.24: Graphical representation of variable contribution

Now click the second option under MODEL REPRESENTATION ![icon]. This is the model accuracy function. You will see a few graphs, as shown in Figure 4.25.

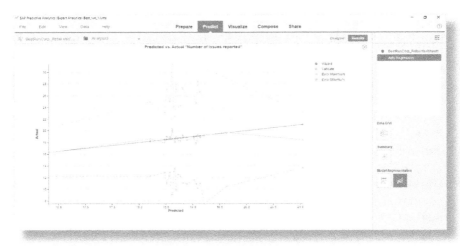

Figure 4.25: More graphical outputs of regression

So what do these graphs mean to a data scientist or a business analyst? These visualizations provide the data scientist or the business analyst both an „at-a-glace" and fact-based means to measure regression. By clicking on the circles/dots on one or more of the graphs, you will be able to find the difference between the predicted values and some other measure such as error maximum or error minimum.

Now let us shift attention from defects to profits. Let's learn more about the correlation between certain (contributing) variables to the profit and their correlation. Why? One of the primary goals of sales and pipeline analysis is to maximize profit, so it is important to understand cause and effect. Figure 4.26 shows how to set this up.

Figure 4.26: Supplying parameters for variable correlation analysis

Flag the following fields as contributing variables: manager, quantity sold, discount, and customer satisfaction. The target variable is profit, of course. Give a name to the new/predicted column. Click DONE to run the algorithm. Once you get a success message, such as the one shown in Figure 4.27, you are ready to consume the results.

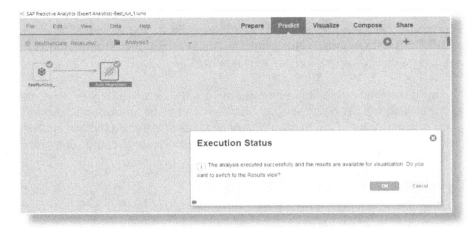

Figure 4.27: Notification of successful completion of analysis

Go the variable contribution view under MODEL REPRESENTATION, as shown in Figure 4.28.

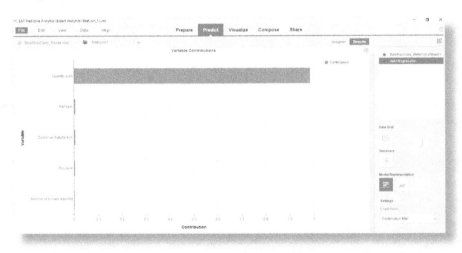

Figure 4.28: Viewing the variable contribution of latest set of contributory input variables

What are the key takeaways?

▶   The only variable that has an impact—and in quite an overwhelming manner—is quantity sold. Its contribution to the profit margin is

98%. The data is saying that sales managers need to focus predominantly on generating sales volumes.

▶ Other variables seem to have very little effect on profit. In fact, surprisingly, the number of issues encountered seems to have the least effect out of all the variables selected. Prior to this, my hypothesis was that the number of issues encountered would have a large impact on the profit margin. But that is not the case. The number of issues encountered is statistically insignificant. This could lead to interesting interpretations, with some being counter-intuitive. You could surmise that you should not focus on quality since the number of issues reported is making such a small impact to the profit margin. You should therefore use various combinations of variables to get a complete picture.

▶ The manager of the sales territory has the second highest correlation to profit from the list of variables at .05%.

Now analyze how other variables contribute to the profit. Since a suspicion still lurks that the contribution made by the number of issues to profit is somewhat understated, retain the number of issues, the manager, and customer satisfaction, but exclude the quantity sold. We already know how closely correlated the quantity sold is to profit. Save the information and run the algorithm. Display the contribution analysis. This is shown in Figure 4.29.

Figure 4.29: Exploring contribution of another set of variables

This graphic reveals interesting results. The manager variable contributes 88% to profit while customer satisfaction is at 7% and number of issues reported is at 5%. These results provide additional validation that the number of issues reported indeed has little correlation to profit. But surprisingly, customer satisfaction is way less important than the sales manager. So from a sales planning perspective it is clear that buyers tend to trust the seller/manager regardless of customer satisfaction and number of issues reported. It also means that by providing the sales managers with all available tools, the company can increase its sales based on the trust that these individuals have earned.

4.1.3   Inter-quartile range

Now let's do some outlier analysis.

What is outlier analysis?

 Outlier analysis is a commonly used technique in statistical analysis. It is also very popular in data mining and predictive analytics. The simplest way to understand this concept is to think of it as a measure for abnormal behavior in a data set. Some extreme values tend to skew the measurement of central tendency in a data set; you can choose to ignore them or incorporate them.

Drag and drop the INTER QUARTILE RANGE algorithm from the right panel and connect it to the output of auto regression. This is shown in Figure 4.30.

Now double-click the INTER QUARTILE RANGE activity on the canvas. This will display the screen shown in Figure 4.31.

Figure 4.30: Getting ready to apply inter quartile range algorithm to data set

Figure 4.31: Parameters for running inter quartile range

The output mode has two options, SHOW OUTLIERS and REMOVE OUT-LIERS. We want to see the the outliers, so select the former option. In the next section, COLUMN SELECTION, you can select the feature (or field) whose outlying values you would like to see. Select the NUMBER OF ISSUES REPORTED from the drop-down.

The next section is BEHAVIOR, where you will assign a fence coefficient for the analysis.

Understanding a box plot

 A common visual tool for outlier analysis is the box plot. A box plot has the median of your data set at the center and at the 25th and the 75th percentiles as Quartile 1 (Q1) and Quartile 3 (Q3) respectively. The value/distance between the quartiles is called the inter-quartile range. The fence coefficient helps in identifying extreme values. Setting it at the default of 1.5 means that any value less than (Q1—1.5 times the IQ range) will be a mild outlier and any value greater than (Q3 + 1.5 times the IQ range) will also be a mild outlier. The same fence coefficient is also used to measure extreme outliers. The corresponding formulas are (Q1—3 times the IQ range) and (Q3 + 3 times the IQ range).

Finally, name your predicted column. Upon clicking DONE and then GO, you will receive a message that the results have been successfully calculated (if you do not have any errors). Go back to PREDICT mode and click the SUMMARY button. It will display your information about outliers and quartiles, as shown in Figure 4.32.

So now we know that there are 237 outliers in our data set of over 16,000 records. The implication is that these can skew any predictive analytics we do.

Unfortunately, there isn't any additional prebuilt visual content for your outlier analysis, so you need to build your own visualization. This is quite straightforward. Switch to the VISUALIZE view and then from drop-down for ANALYSIS TARGETS, select the INTER QUARTILE RANGE option, as shown in Figure 4.33.

Figure 4.32: Summary of outlier analysis

Figure 4.33: Getting ready to visualize results

Choose a chart type to visualize the outlier analysis. There are many options to choose from and it is entirely your prerogative as to which chart type you choose. As I like to say, it's both a science and an art. The science part comes into play when you are trying to choose your measures, dimensions, etc., and the art part becomes relevant when you are trying to make your visualization accentuate your analysis.

Select an area chart for this analysis. To see outliers per country, for example, drag and drop the appropriate fields into MEASURES and DIMENSIONS, as shown in Figure 4.34.

147

Figure 4.34: Identifying the measure and dimensions for visualization

To identify outliers, use the generated column for outliers as the legend color. So what patterns and/or messages are embedded in this chart from a predictive standpoint? France is the only country with outliers so it is definitely worth investigating. Now drill down into cities in France to determine where these large variances in issues reported are coming from.

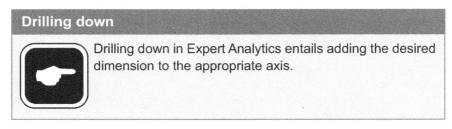

Drilling down

Drilling down in Expert Analytics entails adding the desired dimension to the appropriate axis.

Click "+" in the X AXIS and select CITY. The screen will be similar to what is shown in Figure 4.35.

As you mouse-over each of the four dots atop the green area, the application will display the name of the city and the number of outliers. This is shown in Figure 4.36.

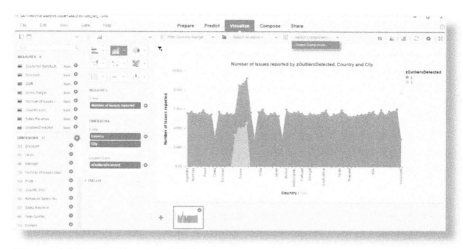

Figure 4.35: Results of a drill-down

Figure 4.36: Browsing cities of interest

As you mouse-over the green peaks, you will see the cities that these outliers occurred in. One of these cities is Paris. So what do these results mean? Basically, it means that for now it is worth investigating why only these four cities in the entire (global) data set have outliers. For the future, it means that corrective measures need to be implemented (based on the current investigation) to ensure that these outliers are minimized, or eliminated, if possible.

4.1.4   Auto classification

Now that you have seen regression, it should be easier to understand classification. It is one of the most popular predictive analytics techniques. A classification algorithm evaluates the data set, taking into account the contributing variables and then providing its predictions (values) in the response variable. The input data set is also commonly known as the *training set* because it is helping the algorithm get better at making predictions. The ultimate goal of classification is to group together similar behavior and to target items in a more specific manner. The output or target variable has to be binary (typically yes or no) in nature. You cannot set a continuous variable as the target of auto classification. Once you select the appropriate target variable, the program determines the appropriate algorithm to use. Based on the combination of input variables, auto classification then decides whether the target variable will have a yes or a no answer. This is where the predictive nature of auto classification resides.

4.1.5   Triple exponential smoothing

If you are not a data scientist and/or are not very familiar with statistical analysis, the term *triple exponential smoothing* may sound geeky.

Exponential smoothing is a popular type of time-series analysis. It belongs to a class of functions known as *window functions* that help in reducing the unevenness of data and provide a smoothing effect. This technique is quite popular in doing trend analysis and forecasting. Instead of using simple (linear) moving average calculations, exponential functions are applied to the input variables with decreasing weights over time. You might infer that exponential smoothing is used in signal processing to minimize *noise*.

Let's look at a practical example of exponential smoothing –weather forecasting. There are considerable variations in daily temperatures from day to day. You can extrapolate based on this daily data, but at the same time reduce the *noise* of these daily variations. The most common technique is to compute a moving average of say, 14 days. This same concept can be applied to many other areas, such as sales demand and pipeline fore-casting. To make sales forecasts based on available data while minimizing outliers and short-term variations, employ a *smoothing factor* (a percent-age) that assigns the highest weight to the most recent period and ex-ponentially decreasing weights to past periods. You will arrive at future projections that minimize the impact of *noise*.

Since this is not a book on data mining, I will skip explanations of single and double exponential smoothing and jump straight to triple exponential smoothing, since this is one of the algorithm options SAP PA provides. Triple exponential smoothing is used when data shows seasonality. Quite simply, it applies exponential smoothing thrice to make the data as smooth as possible.

Now switch to some actual triple exponential smoothing in SAP PA. Since our data set is ready, let's leverage it and apply the exponential algorithm to this existing data set. Drag the algorithm and drop it on the canvas, as shown in Figure 4.37.

Figure 4.37: Getting ready to apply exponential smoothing to a data set

Double-click the button for the exponential algorithm to get a pop-up win-dow where you provide the input variables to the algorithm. See Figure 4.38.

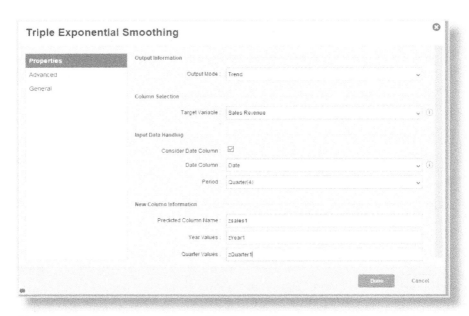

Figure 4.38: Parameters for configuring a triple exponential smoothing run

Let's understand what each of these means. You can select either TREND or FORECAST as the OUTPUT MODE. Let's start with trend analysis. You select one variable as your TARGET VARIABLE. Select SALES REVENUE since we are doing sales forecasting and pipeline analysis. Note that the target variable must be numeric. This is easy to understand—the algorithm outputs numbers so text variables will not work.

In the INPUT DATA HANDLING section, check the CONSIDER DATE COLUMN box so that SAP PA will not take into account the date field and data in the data set. Then specify the date field as the date column. Note that this field must be populated with a date-type field. If you specify a field of any other data type, you cannot run the algorithm. You also need to indicate what periodic data is taken into account (based on your date field). The options are monthly, quarterly, and yearly. Which option you choose is based on how granular the smoothing needs to be. Obviously, quarterly data will inherently contain fewer variations than monthly, but more varations than yearly data. Choose QUARTER as the PERIOD.

Now you need to assign names to the columns/fields that the algorithm will generate. SAP PA inputs default names, but you are free to change them.

Now navigate to the ADVANCED menu item and see what parameters are available and/or need to be changed. This is shown in Figure 4.39.

Figure 4.39: Setting values of important variables

So, what exactly are ALPHA, BETA, and GAMMA? These are constants applied to the input data.

▶ **Alpha**: It is known as the smoothing constant and can be any value between 0 and 1. The closer it is to 1, the faster the smoothing occurs. The single exponential smoothing method does not use the beta or gamma variables.

▶ **Beta**: It is the trend factor and is the output of the double exponential method. It has a value between 0 and 1. Gamma variable is not used in the double exponential method.

▶ **Gamma**: It is a constant which is correlated to alpha and has a value between 0 and 1.

Stick to the defaults, click DONE. If all your variables and values pass the background checks that SAP PA makes, a checkbox appears on the applicable button. You are now ready to run the algorithm by clicking the green arrow button, as shown outlined by a red box in Figure 4.40.

Figure 4.40: Getting ready to run triple exponential smoothing

Once the the algorithm is executed, you should receive a confirmation message, as shown in Figure 4.41.

Figure 4.41: Notification of success of algorithm execution

Click OK. The results display in a data grid by default. This is shown in Figure 4.42.

These results may not be of much analytical use if not displayed in a visual manner. Let's look at the summary of the algorithm run, first. This might be of interest if you are statistically minded. But for business users, a visual output will be more useful. Let's look at some key summary statistics of this job. Click SUMMARY. See Figure 4.43.

Figure 4.42: Tabular view of results of algorithm run

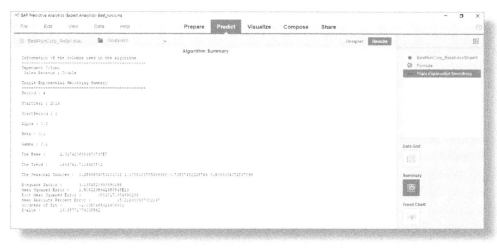

Figure 4.43: Summary of results of algorithm run

You can review the parameters and the computed values. Of interest to the data scientist will be the values at the bottom of the screen.

Switch to the visual analysis by clicking TREND CHART. It will display the screen shown in Figure 4.44.

Figure 4.44: Analyzing the results from the algorithm run

The blue bars show the actual sales revenue and the green line shows the predicted revenue. Based on the inputs and the algorithm, the number of quarters for which actual sales revenue exceeded the predicted sales revenue roughly equals the number of quarters for which the predicted sales revenue exceeded the actual sales revenue. A slightly troubling recent trend seems to be that for the most recent four quarters, the actual sales revenue is below the predicted sales revenue in three of these quarters, with the most recent quarter below by about $6 million. This amounts to nearly 35% of the actual sales generated in Q4.

Now switch to sales forecast. Change the output mode to FORECAST, as shown in Figure 4.45.

The PERIODS TO PREDICT field expects you to provide the number of periods for which you want a prediction to be made. The number of periods is automatically derived from the PERIOD field a few rows below. Set it to quarterly. The target variable remains the same. Give the new columns new names and click DONE. You will see a grid/table view of the results, as shown in the partial screenshot in Figure 4.46.

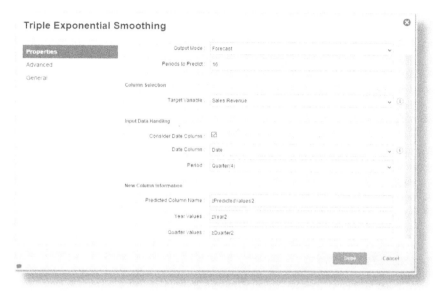

Figure 4.45: Supplying parameters for a forecast smoothing

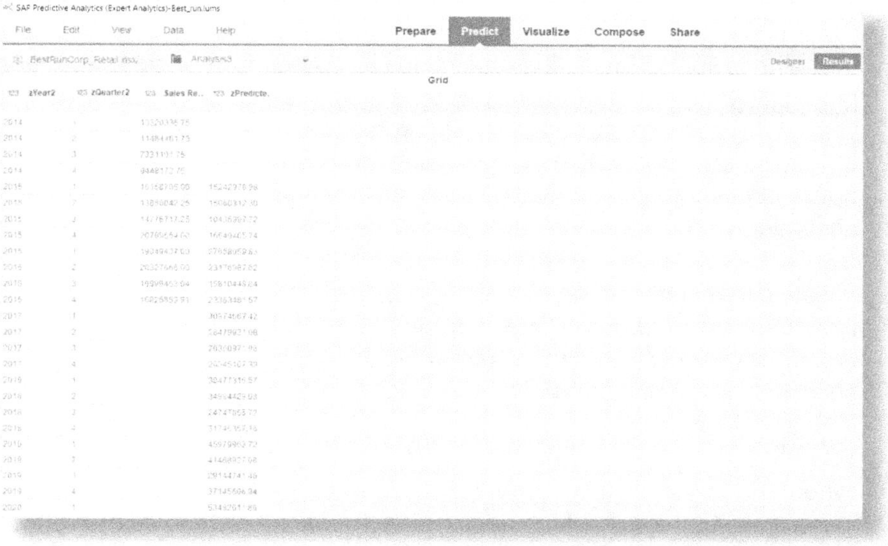

Figure 4.46: Tabular display of smoothing forecast results

Although this may not be of too much value (in tabular format), at a quick glance you can see that the exponential algorithm has generated predicted sales values for the next 16 quarters. Switch to the trend display. This is shown in Figure 4.47.

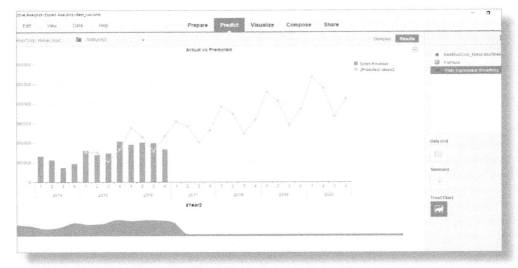

Figure 4.47: Sales forecast for the next 16 periods

What predictive analysis can you do and inferences can you make from the trend graph? Clearly, the projections look good from a general growth perspective. It shows that sales volume is forecasted to increase steadily year over year. From a quarterly standpoint, there is a dip going from Q1 to Q2 and then from Q2 to Q3, but sales finishes the year strong before an uptick in the first quarter. Sales managers can use this information to plan accordingly.

In sales, revenue is not the only KPI sales managers are interested in. The Holy Grail is profit. So let's see trends and forecasts for profit. Change the TARGET VARIABLE to PROFIT and keep everything else the same. After successfully running the algorithm, switch to the trend chart. This is shown in Figure 4.48.

When you compare this graph with that of the sales revenue trend chart in Figure 4.47 there is a high degree of correlation between sales revenue and profit. Although this might sound as a no-brainer, this is not always the case.

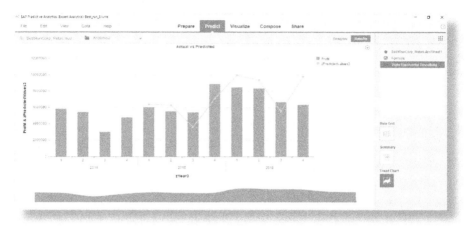

Figure 4.48: Trend chart for actual versus forecast analysis

Now switch to the profit forecast. In the PARAMETERS window, change the output mode to FORECAST and continue with a forecast for 16 periods. Save the information and run the algorithm. Upon successful completion, the application generates a visual output, as shown in Figure 4.49.

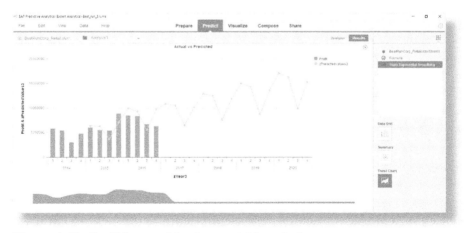

Figure 4.49: Profit forecast for the next 16 periods

159

5 Conclusion

We have reached the end of the journey in your introduction to SAP Predictive Analytics. In the course of the previous four chapters, I strove to provide you with information that is necessary for you to not only stoke your interest in SAP PA but also to take your first steps. It goes without saying that SAP PA is not an easy topic to comprehend since it has a lot of algorithm underlying it. But in recent years it has become sufficiently commoditized and simplified for regular users (defined by those who are not data scientist or statisticians) to leverage. It has therefore been my endeavor to demystify SAP PA so that you, as a regular user, can utilize it. Of course, even as a data scientist, I'm sure you found this book useful.

In Chapter 1, I took you through the genesis of SAP Predictive Analytics and provided you with a historical perspective on it.

In Chapter 2, I provided you with a high-level overview of SAP PA including an introduction, history, and evolution of SAP PA; and the architectural underpinnings and technical components that comprise SAP PA. I also took a detour into the world of SAP HANA and provided you with a commentary on how SAP PA works with SAP HANA. I ended the chapter with a discussion on SAP PA in SAP's Business Intelligence/Analytics roadmap and guided you through the installation steps.

I devoted a large portion of this book to Chapter 3. Here I dove right into the modules and components of SAP PA. The perspective for this chapter was that of the business/end user. Wherever it made sense, I provided you with examples and illustrations of specific components or functions or SAP PA algorithms.

In Chapter 4, I picked a specific use case, that of sales and pipeline forecasting, and selected specific SAP PA functions and algorithms to demonstrate how you can realize this use case.

In closing, I would like to emphasize that the tsunami of data mining, machine learning, and predictive analysis is flattening all our traditional models of historical analysis and making us smarter by providing us with the wherewithal to look into the future with affordable but powerful technology. This will continue to bring profound change to the way we think, plan, and analyze and help align our efforts with the goals and objectives that we have set out to achieve.

It was a privilege for me to write this book on a topic that is near and dear to my heart. In doing so, if I was able to pique your interest in this topic, I will have achieved the goal I had set out to achieve.

6 References

6.1 Websites

Official SAP product website

https://www.sap.com/products/predictive-analytics.html

Official SAP product website that provides you with information with release information, product features, pricing, etc.

Free 30-day trial of SAP PA professional edition

https://www.sap.com/cmp/ft/crm-xm17-gtm-1an-papt/index. html?campaigncode=CRM-XH18-PPC-ANAPFFC3&source=PPC-USCA-Analytics-SASAnaPredictiveAnalyticsFreeTrial-GOO&utm_ medium=PPC&utm_source=Google&utm_campaign=SASAnaPredictiveAnal yticsFreeTrial_FC&utm_term=sap_predictive_analytics&gclid=CPmOpI2E6N wCFRqShQodhE0D0g&gclsrc=ds

This link takes you the registration page for a free 30-day trial of SAP PA professional edition. (I highly recommend you take advantage of this offer).

Home page for SAP PA on the SAP Help Portal

https://help.sap.com/viewer/p/SAP_PREDICTIVE_ANALYTICS

This is the home page for SAP PA on the SAP Help Portal. This is where you go for online help, user guides, and scenarios; the Product Availability Matrix (PAM); and links to videos and tutorials.

Blog on the SAP PA app edition

http://blog-sap.com/analytics/2018/02/15/introducing-sap-predictive-analytics-app-edition/

An Introduction to the K-Means Algorithm

http://blog-sap.com/analytics/2018/06/28/an-introduction-to-the-k-means-algorithm/

An introduction to SAP Infinite Insight

https://blogs.sap.com/2014/03/11/sap-infinite-insight-introduction-and-overview/

Useful blog on modeling with SAP Infinite Insight

https://sapbiblog.com/2014/02/24/modeling-with-sap-infinite-insight/

High-level overview of the evolution and components of SAP PA

https://searchbusinessanalytics.techtarget.com/feature/SAP-Predictive-Analytics-software-overview

SAP PA interview

https://www.kdnuggets.com/2016/05/sap-predictive-analytics-interview-sven-bauszus.html

How SAP PA integrates with SAP HANA

https://sapexperts.wispubs.com/An-Introduction-to-SAP-Predictive-Analysis-and-How-It-Integrates-with-SAP-HANA

An article on how SAP PA integrates with SAP HANA.

Create powerful applications with SAP HANA PAL

https://www.udemy.com/introduction-to-predictive-analytics-on-sap-hana/

An introductory course on Udemy on how to use the SAP HANA PAL to create powerful applications. Note: you need to pay for this online course.

Landing page for the SAP Predictive Analytics community

https://www.sap.com/community/topic/predictive-analytics.html

Some predictions on predictive analytics in the future

https://blogs.sap.com/2018/08/01/what-will-predictive-analytics-look-like-in-2030/

A blog on SAP PA 3.0

https://blogs.sap.com/2016/06/10/the-future-of-sap-predictive-analytics-is-here-with-30/

SAP PA tutorials

https://wiki.scn.sap.com/wiki/pages/viewpage.action?pageId=448476816

This is a Wiki on SAP PA tutorials. It has tutorials for both versions 2.x and 3.x.

SAP Evangelist Timo Elliott

https://timoelliott.com/blog/2013/12/interview-where-is-predictive-analytics-going.html

An older blog article (from 2013), but it contains very good content by SAP Evangelist Timo Elliott.

6.2   YouTube videos

Key advanced features of SAP PA

*https://www.youtube.com/watch?v=uxx-knjkLmw&list=PLkzo92owKnVxlcisdHG-86YSlgyZEtZt_*

On this channel you will find official SAP videos on key advanced features of SAP PA.

What's New in Predictive Analytics 3.3

https://www.youtube.com/watch?v=Cp9-IrgIrvM

SAP Predictive Analytics Industry Use Cases

https://www.youtube.com/watch?v=MyGAAxTFTts

Quickly Preparing Data for Predictive Modeling

https://www.youtube.com/watch?v=F-OCrM04D5l

Automated predictive library

https://www.youtube.com/watch?v=gtAj5JECSG0

Enabling SAP Predictive Analytics Suite for HANA with the Automated Predictive Library

Inside SAP Predictive Analytics 3.x

https://www.youtube.com/watch?v=94ZJUw32pSk

Integrating SAP Predictive Analytics with SAP BW/4HANA and SAP BPC

https://www.youtube.com/watch?v=zyGky3cRHEA

Create a classification / regression model: SAP Predictive Analytics 2.0

https://www.youtube.com/watch?v=AHLfyB-u2Xk

SAP Predictive Analytics 3.3 Webinar Replay: What's New

https://www.youtube.com/watch?v=Rt16MxuZa8U

SAP Predictive Analytics—Expert Analytics Time Series

https://www.youtube.com/watch?v=qCg8qt8bODA

SAP IT Operations Analytics with SAP Predictive Analytics Demo

https://www.youtube.com/watch?v=6x2J1FMXMy0

Gaining Productivity and Profitability with Predictive Analytics

https://www.youtube.com/watch?v=aMqIcvXGEPE

Fraud alerts and SAP Fraud Management

https://www.youtube.com/watch?v=Fj_gUUvSFqo

Increasing Accuracy of Fraud Alerts with SAP Predictive Analytics and SAP Fraud Management

Smart finance through advanced analytics

https://www.youtube.com/watch?v=0BWl2_63tj8

SAP Predictive Analytics: Enabling Smart Finance Through Advanced Analytics

Extend the value of SAP BW/4HANA

https://www.youtube.com/watch?v=WPoES_Oid_g

How SAP Predictive Analytics Extends the Value of SAP BW/4HANA

Expert series on SAP Predictive Analytics

https://www.youtube.com/watch?v=M2f-NgiYmJM&list=PLufF7pZxICBiB8RX AczjhA-rtUp9SAzXi

SAP Predictive Analytics: Ensemble Modelling—A Predictive Modelling Technique

You have finished the book.

A The Author

Anurag Barua is an SAP expert and currently works in the Business Transformation Services (BTS) group at SAP. He has 25 years of experience in conceiving, designing, managing, and implementing complex software solutions, including more than 20 years of experience with SAP applications. He has led enterprise-wide business and digital transformation programs using SAP across nearly 30 enterprises globally and a broad swathe of industry verticals including Public Sector, Media, Manufacturing, Utilities, Financial Services, and Pharmaceuticals. In the last couple of years, Anurag has been heavily involved in advising and leading SAP S/4HANA digital transformation programs for his global clients.

His core SAP competencies include FI and controlling; logistics; SAP BW; SAP BusinessObjects; enterprise performance management (EPM); SAP Solution Manager; SAP Fiori; governance, risk, and compliance (GRC); and project management. He is a frequent speaker at SAP conferences globally and contributes to several publications. He has written three books on SAP, including *First Steps in SAP Fiori* for Espresso Tutorials. He holds a Bachelor of Science in Computer Science and an MBA in Finance. He is a PMI-certified PMP, a Certified Scrum Master (CSM), and is ITIL V3F certified. You may contact Anurag via email at Anurag.barua@gmail.com.

B Index

A

Analysis Process Designer 21
Analytical computing 12
Application function library 26
Artificial intelligence 21
Automated Analytics 20

B

Big Data 16
Box plot 146

C

Classification 50
cloud computing 15
Clustering 68, 132
Cutting Strategy 55

D

Data Manager 35
Data scientists 20
Decision support systems 12
Decision Tree 82
Drill down 148

E

ERP 14
ETL 25
Expert Analytics 20

G

Grid computing 15

I

Infinite Insight 20
Infographic 103
Inter-quartile range 144

K

Knowledge economy 21

L

Line charts 97
Lumira 24

M

Machine learning 21
Modeler 49
Moore's Law 13, 15

N

Neural networks 82

O

Outlier analysis 144
Outliers 82

P

Partition 94
Pie Charts 98
Predictive analytical library 25

R

Regression 50, 137

S

Sales/pipeline forecasting 125
SAP Analytics Cloud 29
SAP Cloud Platform 25
SAP HANA 23
Scatter Charts 99

T

Text analysis 43
Triple exponential smoothing 150

C Disclaimer

This publication contains references to the products of SAP SE.

SAP, R/3, SAP NetWeaver, Duet, PartnerEdge, ByDesign, SAP Business-Objects Explorer, StreamWork, and other SAP products and services mentioned herein as well as their respective logos are trademarks or registered trademarks of SAP SE in Germany and other countries.

Business Objects and the Business Objects logo, BusinessObjects, Crystal Reports, Crystal Decisions, Web Intelligence, Xcelsius, and other Business Objects products and services mentioned herein as well as their respective logos are trademarks or registered trademarks of Business Objects Software Ltd. Business Objects is an SAP company.

Sybase and Adaptive Server, iAnywhere, Sybase 365, SQL Anywhere, and other Sybase products and services mentioned herein as well as their respective logos are trademarks or registered trademarks of Sybase, Inc. Sybase is an SAP company.

SAP SE is neither the author nor the publisher of this publication and is not responsible for its content. SAP Group shall not be liable for errors or omissions with respect to the materials. The only warranties for SAP Group products and services are those that are set forth in the express warranty statements accompanying such products and services, if any. Nothing herein should be construed as constituting an additional warranty.

More Espresso Tutorials Books

Wolfgang Niefert:

Business Intelligence with SAP® BI Edge

- ▶ Get to know the BI Edge Solutions 4.1
- ▶ Universe, Crystal Reports and Web Intelligence for beginners
- ▶ Learn about Connecting BI with SAP ERP (ECC 6.0)
- ▶ Case study with many screenshots and explanations

http://4040.espresso-tutorials.com

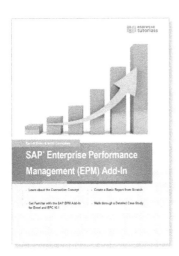

Kermit Bravo & Scott Cairncross:

SAP® Enterprise Performance Management (EPM) Add-In

- ▶ Learn about the Connection Concept
- ▶ Get familiar with the SAP EPM Add-In for Excel and BPC 10.1
- ▶ Create a Basic Report from Scratch
- ▶ Walk through a Detailed Case Study

http://5042.espresso-tutorials.com

Gerardo di Giuseppe:

First Steps in SAP® Business Warehouse (BW)

► Tips for Loading Data to SAP BW with SAP ETL

► Using Business Content to Accelerate your BW objects

► How to Automate ETL Tasks Using Process Chains

► Leverage BEx Query Designer and BEx Analyzer

http://5088.espresso-tutorials.com

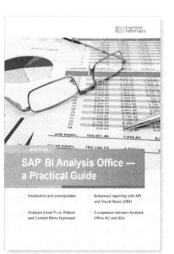

Jörg Böke:

SAP® BI Analysis Office – a Practical Guide

► Installation and prerequisites

► Analysis Excel Pivot, Ribbon and Context Menu Explained

► Enhanced reporting with API and Visual Basic (VBA)

► Comparison between Analysis Office AO and BEx

http://5096.espresso-tutorials.com

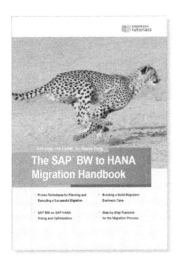

Rob Frye, Joe Darlak, Dr. Bjarne Berg:

The SAP® BW to HANA Migration Handbook

▶ Proven Techniques for Planning and Executing a Successful Migration
▶ SAP BW on SAP HANA Sizing and Optimization
▶ Building a Solid Migration Business Case
▶ Step-by-Step Runbook for the Migration Process

http://5109.espresso-tutorials.com

Christian Savelli:

SAP® BW on SAP HANA

▶ Tips for upgrading, maintaining, and running BW on HANA
▶ Data loading methods and real-time data acquisition
▶ New reporting paradigm for BW on HANA
▶ HANA data architecture

http://5128.espresso-tutorials.com

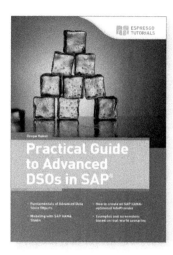

Deepa Rawat:

Practical Guide to Advanced DSOs in SAP®

▶ Fundamentals of Advanced Data Store Objects

▶ Modeling with SAP HANA Studio

▶ How to create an SAP HANA-optimized InfoProvider

▶ Examples and screenshots based on real-world scenarios

http://5213.espresso-tutorials.com

Frank Riesner, Klaus-Peter Sauer:

SAP® BW/4HANA and BW on HANA

▶ Migration, sizing, operation, data management with SAP BW/4HANA and SAP BW 7.5 on HANA

▶ The new central source Systems SAP HANA and ODP

▶ New modeling options, mixed scenarios, LSA++, and differences compared to SAP BW 7.5

▶ The role of BW in operational SAP reporting

http://5215.espresso-tutorials.com

www.ingramcontent.com/pod-product-compliance
Lightning Source LLC
LaVergne TN
LVHW022318060326
832902LV00020B/3535